ASIAN ARGUMENTS

Asian Arguments is a series of short books about Asia today. Aimed at the growing number of students and general readers who want to know more about the region, these books will highlight community involvement from the ground up in issues of the day usually discussed by authors in terms of top-down government policy. The aim is to better understand how ordinary Asian citizens are confronting problems such as the environment, democracy and their societies' development, either with or without government support. The books are scholarly but engaged, substantive as well as topical, and written by authors with direct experience of their subject matter.

ABOUT THE AUTHOR

ANDREW MACGREGOR MARSHALL is a journalist, political risk consultant and corporate investigator, focusing mainly on Southeast Asia. He spent seventeen years as a correspondent for Reuters, covering conflicts in, among others, Iraq, Afghanistan and Pakistan, and political upheaval in Thailand. Marshall resigned from Reuters in 2011 after the news agency refused to publish his analysis of leaked US cables illuminating the role played by Thailand's monarchy in the political conflict that has engulfed the kingdom. A fugitive from Thai law as a result of his journalism about the royal family, he now lives in Phnom Penh.

A KINGDOM IN CRISIS

Thailand's struggle for democracy
in the twenty-first century

ANDREW MacGREGOR MARSHALL

Zed Books | LONDON

A Kingdom in Crisis: Thailand's Struggle for Democracy in the Twenty-First Century was first published in 2014 by Zed Books Ltd,
7 Cynthia Street, London N1 9JF, UK

www.zedbooks.co.uk

Copyright © Andrew MacGregor Marshall 2014

The right of Andrew MacGregor Marshall to be identified as
the author of this work has been asserted by him in accordance
with the Copyright, Designs and Patents Act, 1988

Designed and typeset in Monotype Bulmer by illuminati, Grosmont
Index by John Barker
Cover designed by www.alice-marwick.co.uk

All rights reserved. No part of this publication may be
reproduced, stored in a retrieval system or transmitted in any
form or by any means, electronic, mechanical, photocopying or
otherwise, without the prior permission of Zed Books Ltd.

A catalogue record for this book is available from the British Library
Library of Congress Cataloging in Publication Data available

ISBN 978-1-78360-058-8 hb
ISBN 978-1-78360-057-1 pb
ISBN 978-1-78360-059-5 pdf
ISBN 978-1-78360-060-1 epub
ISBN 978-1-78360-061-8 mobi

MIX
Paper from
responsible sources
FSC
www.fsc.org FSC® C013604

Printed and bound by CPI Group (UK) Ltd, Croydon, CR0 4YY

Contents

Acknowledgements

A great many people have provided me with immense support and assistance during this project, on both a professional and a personal level. The book could not have even begun to be written without their help. Sadly, given the possible consequences of breaking Thailand's taboos, it might put them in danger to thank them here. My debt to many superb scholars of Thailand is evident from the citations of their work throughout the book. My thanks to those people who have given me particular help will have to be expressed in private for now. But, above all, it is important to salute the team at Zed Books, in particular Asian Arguments editor Paul French and commissioning editor Kim Walker, for taking the courageous decision to publish *A Kingdom in Crisis* and for so graciously and patiently putting up with my infuriating working habits and missed deadlines. Responsibility for any errors, and for the opinions I express, is mine alone.

A note on names

Thai names can be spelled in multiple ways in English. There is no universally accepted system of transliteration, and English-language spellings sometimes bear no relation to how Thai names are pronounced. This book uses the most commonly used spellings for public figures and historical personalities. When there is no consensus, it uses the spelling that conforms most closely to phonetic pronunciation.

Thailand was commonly known as Siam by foreigners until 1939, when it changed its name. It reverted back to its old name from 1946 until 1949.

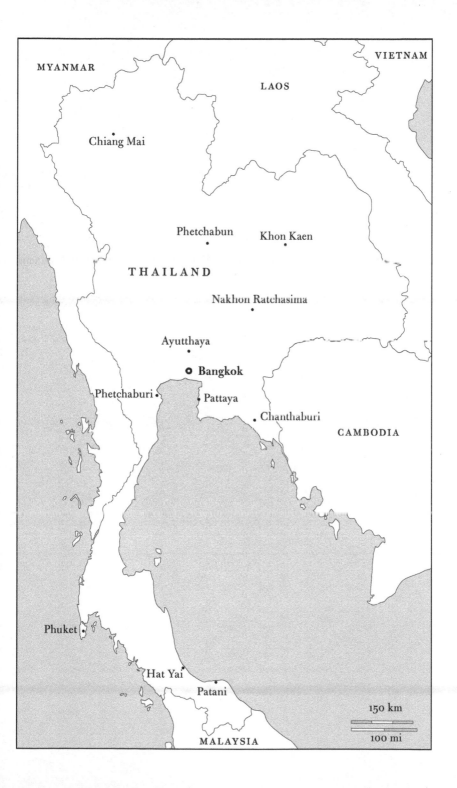

INTRODUCTION

Telling the truth about Thailand

Twenty-first-century Thailand is convulsed by an intractable political conflict that nobody seems able to explain. The traditional ruling class is locked in a destructive battle to crush the political influence of former telecommunications tycoon Thaksin Shinawatra, the most popular prime minister in Thai history, who lives abroad in self-imposed exile after being overthrown in a coup in 2006 and convicted of corruption in 2008. The escalating crisis has inflicted severe collateral damage on Thailand, enfeebling the economy, eroding the quality of governance, and undermining the rule of law. Yet there appears to be no end in sight. Instead of seeking compromise and reconciliation, Thailand's political, business and military elite seem hell-bent on securing absolute victory whatever the cost.

Hanging over the increasingly divided country is the looming trauma of the death of the widely revered Bhumibol Adulyadej, King Rama IX of the Chakri dynasty, who has reigned as monarch since 1946. For decades, most Thais and foreign observers have been convinced that the royal succession and its aftermath will be a particularly perilous period. A stark indication of this anxiety was the collapse in the Thai stock market in October 2009 on rumours that Bhumibol's health had deteriorated. The main index lost 7 per cent over two days, wiping US$13 billion off share prices.

But the accepted wisdom is that succession has little to do with the current political struggle, because it is assumed there is no significant conflict over who will be the next monarch. The king's only son, Crown Prince Maha Vajiralongkorn, is widely expected to become Rama X when Bhumibol dies. Most academic and journalistic analysis of Thailand's conflict leaves out the succession altogether, and foreign correspondents often struggle to characterize exactly what is going on and why – 'Thailand's political turmoil defies concise explanation', according to Thomas Fuller of the *New York Times* (Fuller, 2014). Some observers acknowledge that succession concerns play a part in the conflict because the traditional elite are alarmed about the prospect of Thaksin being in control of parliament when the transition from Bhumibol to Vajiralongkorn takes place. Paul Handley, whose biography *The King Never Smiles* is among the bravest and most illuminating works on Thailand's modern history, made this argument after the 2006 coup: 'There was a clear meeting of minds between the crown and the military ... that they did not want Thaksin in a position to exert influence on the passing of the Chakri Dynasty mantle to Crown Prince Vajiralongkorn' (Handley, 2006b).

But viewed in these terms, much about Thailand's chronic political conflict simply doesn't make sense. Why is the royalist establishment so desperate to prevent Thaksin influencing the succession if it is a foregone conclusion that the crown prince will become the next monarch? Why have they done so little to prepare the ground for an orderly transition? Given the widespread concern that Bhumibol's death will be profoundly destabilizing, why have the elite relentlessly roiled Thailand with their struggle against Thaksin when surely they should be seeking to calm the turbulence? What makes Thaksin so different from and more dangerous than all the corrupt political strongmen in the past whom the palace and establishment found a way to work with? Why are some royalists allied with Thaksin? And why are the traditionally pragmatic and unprincipled Thai elite so implacably opposed to finding some accommodation with him, and obsessed with wild notions of impending catastrophe and existential doom? Most journalism and academic research on Thailand struggles to answer these questions.

This book argues that the consensus is wrong. An unacknowledged conflict over royal succession is at the heart of Thailand's twenty-first century political crisis. More than three decades ago, in a game-changing analysis, Benedict Anderson coolly overturned decades of accepted wisdom and showed that many of the most cherished assumptions of scholars were entirely incorrect. He proposed four 'scandalous hypotheses' that profoundly redefined our understanding of Thai history (Anderson, 1978). In this book, I set out four hypotheses of my own, which I believe are essential to understanding Thailand's turmoil:

1. At the elite level, Thailand's conflict is essentially a succession struggle over who will become monarch when King Bhumibol dies. In particular, most of Thailand's elite are implacably opposed to the prospect of Vajiralongkorn succeeding his father, and are prepared to go to extreme lengths to sabotage the succession.
2. The assumption that Bhumibol's death will unleash a period of upheaval and instability misses the point that this era has already begun. The long-feared end-reign conflict has been in full swing since 2005.

3. The intense struggle over succession does not imply that the monarch has significant political power as an independent actor. Thai kings have usually been puppets of the elite rather than their masters. The elite want a monarch they can control, which gives them access to the legitimizing sacred aura of the palace and to the immense royal fortune.

4. Most Thais who consider themselves royalists are not really royalist at all. The majority of ordinary Thais are 'Bhumibolists' whose loyalty is not to the institution of the monarchy but to what they perceive to be the values and wishes of the current king. Most of the elite are not even necessarily loyal to Bhumibol but seek to exploit the monarchy to serve their own interests. Their intense ultra-royalism is an act, intended to mask their antipathy to Vajiralongkorn. Thaksin is a conventional elite royalist in important respects – he wants to use the monarchy, not overthrow it. But, unlike most of the elite, Thaksin has no qualms about the crown prince becoming Rama X.

The story of contemporary Thailand's trauma is by no means about succession alone. The broader narrative is another much more significant historic struggle by Thailand's people to free themselves from domination and exploitation by the ruling class. The turbulence in Thailand is best understood in terms of these two entangled conflicts – an unacknowledged war of succession, waged in secret by the country's most powerful people, and a struggle for equality and liberty that encompasses the whole country. Both conflicts pivot on the same issue – the power and privilege of the palace and the elite. A third conflict forms the backdrop to the story: a battle over truth. For centuries, the elite have imposed their own version of reality on Thailand's people, and suppressed competing narratives. Now, the ideology and fairy tales of the ruling class are falling apart. Viewed in terms of these three struggles – over truth, democracy and royal succession – Thailand's bewildering crisis becomes comprehensible.

How could so many people have got it so wrong? The most obvious reason is that telling the truth about Thai history and politics is illegal. Article 112 of the Thai Criminal Code states: 'Whoever defames, insults or threatens the King, Queen, the Heir-apparent or the Regent, shall be punished with imprisonment of three to fifteen years.' In practice the draconian *lèse-majesté* law is interpreted so widely that any public comment about the royal family that strays from the absurdly hagiographical official narrative risks a lengthy prison sentence. 'Never has such an archaic law held such sway over a "modern" society (except perhaps "Muslim" theocracies like Afghanistan under the Taliban)', observes David Streckfuss:

> Thailand's use of the lèse majesté law has become unique in the world and its elaboration and justifications have become an art. The law's defenders claim that Thailand's love and reverence for its king is incomparable. Its critics say the law has become the foremost threat to freedom of expression. Barely hidden beneath the surface of growing debate around the law and its use are the most basic issues defining the relationship between those in power and the governed: equality before the law, rights and liberties, the source of sovereign power, and even the system of government of the polity – whether Thailand is to be primarily a constitutional monarchy, a democratic system of governance with the king as head of state, or a democracy. (Streckfuss, 2011)

Truth is not an accepted defence against *lèse-majesté* charges – the issue is whether a statement has damaged the image of the monarchy, regardless of whether it is accurate. This was made explicit in the trial in 2012 of street vendor Ekachai Hongkang-wan, charged with *lèse-majesté* for selling copies of one of the most incendiary US cables obtained by WikiLeaks, as well as DVDs of an Australian Broadcasting Corporation documentary about the royal family. The banned material dated from 2010 and discussed the taboo issues of royal succession and the elite's doubts about Vajiralongkorn. Ekachai's defence team tried to summon the elder statesmen quoted in the leaked cable to ascertain whether their reported remarks about the crown prince were genuine. Judge Aphisit Veeramitchai told them this was futile: 'Because if it is true, it is more defamatory and if it isn't true, then it's super defamatory', he explained. 'So proving whether the information is factual or not will not be beneficial to you at all' (Pravit, 2012).

As a result, journalists and academics tend to tiptoe around the subject of the monarchy, confining their attentions to less controversial topics or simply repeating the traditional fables. As Streckfuss says:

> The lèse majesté law shields this overwhelming, inescapable presence in Thai society, politics and the economy. As a result, the operation of the lèse majesté law in Thailand creates a black hole of silence in the center of the Thai body politic. Political and social discourse is relegated to the fringes as whisperings and innuendo. (Streckfuss, 2011)

But it is quite simply impossible to explain Thailand's crisis adequately without tackling the elephant in the room, not just because the leading royals frequently enter the fray and explicitly take sides despite being officially above politics, but even more importantly because the Thai crisis is fundamentally *about* the monarchy and its role in society. Anyone writing about contemporary Thailand faces the extraordinary dilemma that telling the truth about the country's recent history or politics can only be done by breaking Thai law.

Foreign journalists have tended to become beguiled by Thailand's fairy tales and intimidated by the repercussions of questioning the official narrative. Their reporting has been woefully inadequate in explaining the political crisis. Thailand's elite have been able to impose their version of reality on the country's people with impunity, jailing people for years simply for expressing their honest opinion or stating objective facts. This book is aimed at helping rectify this situation. It provides an accessible new interpretation of the political crisis that explains the actions and strategy of leading players and allows informed forecasts to be made about Thailand's future. It also seeks to shatter some of the damaging taboos restricting discourse, and push outwards the boundaries of what it is acceptable to say. As Slavoj Žižek argued in an essay on the WikiLeaks 'Cablegate' revelations, uttering taboo truths can have a liberating effect even if many people privately already know them to be true:

> The only surprising thing about the WikiLeaks revelations is that they contain no surprises. Didn't we learn exactly what we expected to learn? The real disturbance was at the level of appearances: we can no longer pretend we don't know what everyone knows we know. This is the paradox of public space: even if everyone knows an unpleasant fact, saying it in public changes everything. (Žižek, 2011)

Hans Christian Andersen made the same point in his parable *The Emperor's New Clothes*. Even if most people privately suspect the truth, putting it in the public domain makes it impossible to sustain official narratives that depend on a refusal to acknowledge the reality.

The book draws heavily on texts from outside the dominant royalist narrative, many of them written by outsiders – accounts of foreign travellers to Thailand through the ages, leaked or declassified US and British cables, and underground seditious Thai documents. Foreign observers bring their own prejudices and agendas to Thailand and their analysis must be treated with caution, but such 'heretical' narratives provide an important antidote to the official myths. Much of the analysis of the past decade is based on interviews with hundreds of highly placed Thai sources who cannot be named for their own safety. This is far from ideal, but there is no other way to report on modern Thailand. The book also devotes considerable space to analysis of the motivations and behaviour of the elite, in apparent contradiction to the ethos of the *Asian Arguments* series. But for Thailand's people to take full control of their destiny and escape the ideological shackles that constrain their freedom, the secretive actions of the Thai ruling class have to be brought fully into the open. The unacknowledged conflict over royal succession is far less significant than the struggle for democracy and equal rights for all of Thailand's people, but investigating and exposing it is essential to provide a full understanding of the kingdom's crisis.

The only way for Thais to solve their tragic political conflict and find a way to heal society's divisions is for the country's people to talk, openly and without fear. I hope this book makes a modest contribution towards enabling that to happen.

PART I

Royalty versus reality

ONE

'When the legends die, all collapses'
Thailand's political awakening

The most momentous event in the history of Thailand's reigning Chakri dynasty since the 1932 revolution that stripped the monarchy of absolute power unfolded quite unexpectedly shortly before dusk on a Sunday evening in September 2010. It occurred in the middle of a Bangkok traffic intersection surrounded by luxury malls and five-star hotels and haunted by restless spirits. It was over within a few minutes, and many Thais remain unaware that it ever happened at all.

The date was 19 September. It was exactly four years since royalist generals had seized power in a coup that snuffed out the precious embers of political progress so many Thais had fought and died for in bloody confrontations in past decades. It was just four months since the military had crushed another mass pro-democracy rally in May, storming the fortified encampment occupied by thousands of 'Red Shirt' protesters who had blockaded the Ratchaprasong intersection in the commercial heart of the capital to demand new elections. After armoured vehicles smashed through the barricades of the protest camp at dawn, scattering the Red Shirts, arsonists set dozens of buildings ablaze around the city, and an inferno consumed much of the Zen department store, part of the Central World mega-mall at Ratchaprasong, sending a thick column of smoke into the sky. By the time it was all over, ninety-one people had been killed in the battles of 2010, most of them unarmed civilians, new casualties of the long struggle over how Thailand should be governed.

In the months that followed, the military-backed government banned political gatherings and did its best to rewrite the narrative of what happened. The deaths were de-emphasized, with official propaganda focusing instead on the arson attacks – the Red Shirts were widely accused of having 'burned Bangkok'. Army chief General Prayuth Chan-ocha made the extraordinary claim that the military had not killed or even wounded a single person during two months of clashes, despite official statistics that showed soldiers had used 117,923 bullets, including 2,500 sniper rounds. Meanwhile, Thais were told to work together to build a better future, not dwell on the divisive quarrels of the past. The gutted shell of the Zen store was concealed behind corrugated metal screens painted with slogans reflecting the official mood of forced optimism and forgetfulness. One repeated, over and over, a single phrase:

EVERYTHING WILL BE OK.
EVERYTHING WILL BE OK.
EVERYTHING WILL BE OK.

Another giant banner proclaimed:

REBUILDING ZEN, LOVING THAILAND
May this Rebuilding Bring Peace and Prosperity to Thailand.
We Must Reconcile as We Are One Country,
One Family and One People.

There was little scope for any organized challenge to this narrative. A state of emergency was enforced in Bangkok and across the Red Shirt heartlands in Thailand's north and north-east.

Almost all of the movement's leaders were in jail or on the run. Dissenting voices were being systematically silenced.

Throughout Thailand's modern history, the state has tried to suppress and deny the sacrifice of those who died fighting for equal rights and democracy. One of the worst massacres in living memory was on 6 October 1976, when thousands of ultra-royalist militiamen and police armed with guns, knives, sticks, rocket-propelled grenades and anti-tank weapons attacked student protesters in the grounds of Thammasat University. An accurate official death toll was never released, but reliable estimates suggest more than 100 students were killed. According to an eyewitness report in *Time* magazine,

> Several were beaten close to death, then hanged, or doused with gasoline and set afire. One was decapitated. The bodies of the lynched victims strung up on trees were mutilated by rioters, who gouged out their eyes, slit their throats and lashed at them with clubs and chains. (Aikman, 1976)

The episode has been virtually erased from history. As Thongchai Winichakul, a student leader in 1976 who spent nearly two years in jail after the massacre, wrote: 'It's as if it never happened, or as if its only value was to teach people how to forget' (Thongchai, 1995). Now one of Thailand's most respected historians, Thongchai warned after the violence of 2010 that the state would again seek to bury the memory of those who died. 'Again, reconciliation without justice is expected', he wrote. 'Soon the lost lives and souls will become faceless names, then eventually statistics. Then their stories will be silenced too' (Thongchai, 2011).

In response to state censorship and suppression, rituals of remembrance have long been central to Thai political resistance, with the photographs of the dead displayed at shrines and monuments, along with offerings of candles, incense, fruit and flowers. As Alan Klima observed in a study of the role of the dead in Thai political ritual: 'Such funeral protest culture has become common for suppressed and hunted people around the world' (Klima, 2002). In the months after the killings of April and May 2010, protesters led by human rights activist Sombat Boonngamanong repeatedly returned to Ratchaprasong to commemorate those who died. The first protest was by Sombat alone – on 26 June he tied red ribbons around a large street sign at the Ratchaprasong intersection. He was arrested, and detained for two weeks. Two days after his release, Sombat went back to Ratchaprasong, with around 30 other protesters who swept through the crowds of Sunday afternoon shoppers and converged on the street sign. Some began fixing red tape and ribbons around the sign; others held up placards printed with the words: 'People died here.' Three protesters daubed in red paint lay on the sidewalk in a symbolic piece of street theatre. Several police were present, but kept their distance, even though political gatherings of more than five people were banned under the state of emergency. The authorities were unsure how to react to protests so deliberately small and non-confrontational. On 25 July there was a 'Red aerobics' event. Some of those who took part in the exercise session were smeared with fake blood or had painted their faces into grotesque death masks. On 1 August, scores of Red Shirts lay on the ground at the Democracy Monument in memory of the dead. Another aerobics event on 8 August drew more than 500 people; a week later it was 600. On 12 September, Sombat organized a Red bicycle rally in the area around Ratchaprasong, pausing at places where people had been killed during the May violence. Cyclists yelled 'soldiers shot the people' and 'we do not forget' as they pedalled along the streets. Meanwhile, a group of students with ghoulish make-up and torn, bloodied clothes held a procession on foot.

Many dismissed these events as irrelevant, and Sombat was often portrayed in the media as a clown. But they were part of a strategy to expand the possibilities for protest and help potential supporters overcome their fear, ahead of a large rally planned for 19 September 2010. As Sombat told Peter Boyle of the *Green Left Weekly*: 'We organised a process to break down this fear. The build-up events were symbolic appearances that were not big enough to provoke the full force of government' (Boyle, 2010). Having begun less than three months before by going alone to Ratchaprasong and tying a red ribbon, he was now planning a mass gathering of protesters who would release 10,000 red balloons into the sky and tie 100,000 strips of red cloth all around the area.

Sombat was as stunned as everybody else by the massive crowd that gathered on 19 September. The Red Shirt movement was effectively leaderless and was assumed to be disorganized and adrift. But well over 10,000 protesters converged at Ratchaprasong despite bad weather and the risk of arrest. Anger had long been simmering in rural Red Shirt strongholds, and thousands had travelled to Bangkok in buses and cars to join the protest. Thai journalist Pravit Rojanaphruk described the scene in *The Nation* newspaper:

> A 35-year-old woman, Sangwan Suktisen, whose 31-year-old husband Paison Tiplom died on April 10 at Khok Wua intersection, came with her eight-year-old son and three-year-old daughter to join the event.
> She held a picture of her husband, who was shot in the head, to show other red-shirt protesters walking around the intersection.

She said she called for the government to bring to justice the persons who killed her husband.

'Even though the government gave me compensation for the death of my husband, no one apologised', she said. Her three-year-old Saiphan Tiplom held a red balloon with writing: 'Bring my father back and get the government out.'

Sarawut Sathan, 45, who came from Bang Kapi district, said he joined the protest because he wanted the government to dissolve the House and hold fresh elections as a way to resolve the crisis in society. Another woman wrote on the road with chalk that she still remembered the time when her friend was killed four months ago.

Sombat said [the] symbolic activity at Rajprasong had succeeded in getting the government's attention. He said he did not expect that over 10,000 would join the rally. 'We just came here to tell the government that we will never forget', he said. (Pravit, 2010)

Towards the end of the protest, it became clear that everything had changed for Thailand's monarchy. A slogan began to be shouted among one group of protesters and spread through the crowd until hundreds were chanting it over and over again. It was a denunciation, using a colloquial insult that literally means 'monitor lizard', a particularly reviled animal in Thailand; the closest English-language equivalent is probably 'The bastard ordered the killing.' It was a stunning moment, an event most Thais never dreamed would happen. Hundreds of people in the heart of the capital were shouting a crude insult and inflammatory accusation at an unthinkable target. The 'bastard' was King Bhumibol Adulyadej.

Protesters also began scrawling anti-royal graffiti on the enclosure around the ruins of Zen. Serhat Ünaldi describes it as 'a watershed moment in recent Thai history that has remained almost unnoticed in analyses of the country's political crisis':

Writing graffiti on a wall which had been plastered with feel-good messages of unity, harmony and peace after the bloody crackdown

of May 19, 2010 was a means of countering the Bangkok elite's
escapist attempt of return to 'normal'. The symbols of delusion
were overwritten. (Ünaldi, 2013)

The graffiti included multiple references to the sky – a common
euphemism for the out-of-reach realm of royalty. Numerous
slogans also referenced the king's blindness, and one drawing
even caricatured Bhumibol as Adolf Hitler, wearing an eyepatch.
The king lost an eye in a car crash in 1948, but the messages
were also symbolic, inverting the traditional assumption that
the king's lofty position and immense Buddhist merit gave him
special insight into the sacred essence of reality, beyond the realm
of appearances that the vision of ordinary mortals could never
penetrate (Gray, 1986; Ünaldi, 2013). In several messages, the Red
Shirts declared they were the ones who really saw things clearly.
References to sight and blindness were part of a coded semi-secret
language that had developed among opponents of the monarchy,
who called themselves *taa sawang* – meaning their eyes had been
opened. 'Before I used to love you … but now I hate you – go
to ruin! Today Thais everywhere in the country have their eyes
open', wrote one protester. Another scrawled: 'Bad people were
taken to rule the land because heaven has no eyes, because the
eyes are blind… I ask for real, you damn blind man, when will
you die?' (Ünaldi, 2013).

The collapse in support for Thailand's monarchy was stun-
ningly swift. When Bhumibol celebrated his Diamond Jubilee
in June 2006, the elderly monarch was revered by most Thais
and admired around the globe as a visionary leader who had
fused ancient tradition and modern statecraft to forge a stable
democratic nation. Five days of royal pageantry marked the occasion, amid an outpouring of adoration from Thailand's people

and an impressive show of respect from world leaders. All over the country, Thais dressed in yellow to honour Bhumibol, and wore rubber wristbands with the slogan 'Long Live the King'. On 9 June, a million people crowded into Bangkok's Royal Plaza to see Bhumibol give a public address – only his third in six decades – from a palace balcony. Later that day, at the auspicious time of 19:19, hundreds of thousands of Thais who had gathered around the brightly illuminated buildings of the Grand Palace lit candles in his honour. On 12 June, the assembled international heads of state were treated to the unforgettable sight of a royal barge procession – 2,082 liveried oarsmen rowed fifty-two sleek vessels up the Chao Phraya river to Wat Arun, the temple of the dawn. Bhumibol sat aboard his personal swan-headed vessel *Suphannahongse*, representing the mythical bird ridden by the Hindu god Brahma. In a confidential cable describing the sixtieth anniversary celebrations, US ambassador Ralph 'Skip' Boyce seemed awed by the occasion:

> The multi-day gala offered dramatic and often times moving evidence of the nation's respect and adoration for its monarch…
>
> Bangkok's sidewalks and public transportation became a sea of yellow, as citizens donned the color of the King's birthday (a Monday, thus a yellow day.) The rush to conform even found expression on the local markets, where the price of yellow 'we love the King' shirts skyrocketed. In response, the government announced that it would produce extra shipments of such clothing, to force down the price. Bangkok's normally snarled traffic reached new heights of obstruction, with motorcades and security details turning local roads into parking lots. While government offices and schools were closed, the malls and markets remained open; the sound of radio and television broadcasts of the gala filling the air.
>
> The local press focused exclusively on the celebration. Newspapers carried full-page sections on the King's life and works. Interviews with Thai of all ages and backgrounds conveyed the same joyous appreciation for the monarch, with individual stories

of how royal assistance had improved their lives. All local television stations carried the same live feed of each event, which featured crowd shots of attendees alternately crying and smiling. Late night television shifted to cover the opening of the World Cup, but even this event was colored by the King's celebration: a newspaper cartoon explained that most Thai people were cheering for Brazil because the Brazilians wear yellow uniforms.

Bhumibol's reputation was at its zenith. But behind the pageantry, the Father of the Nation was struggling with family problems. Bhumibol had been estranged from Queen Sirikit for two decades, and his son and heir, Crown Prince Vajiralongkorn, was regarded as a cruel and corrupt womanizer, reviled by most Thais. The king's second daughter, Princess Sirindhorn, was the overwhelming favourite of the Thai people to succeed her father, even though her gender and royal tradition seemed to render this impossible. As Boyce wrote:

> In a shot heavy with unintentional meaning on Friday, the television broadcast showed the unpopular Crown Prince reading a message of congratulations to the King, who was seated on the royal balcony above the Prince. Just visible behind the King, however, was the smiling face of Princess Sirindhorn – the widely respected 'intellectual heir' of the monarch – chatting with her sisters and trying to take a picture of the adoring crowd below. The physical distance between the King and his legal heir far below, and his beloved daughter just behind him, captured the internal family dynamic – and the future of the monarchy – quite nicely. (06BANGKOK3538)

Most of Thailand's poor still revered Bhumibol, never questioning the official story that he was a wise and caring monarch who had worked tirelessly throughout his reign to improve their lives. They saw him as their guardian and protector, in contrast to corrupt politicians and bureaucrats who had always treated them with disdain and never done anything for them. But they had become ardent supporters of Thaksin Shinawatra after he became prime minister in 2001 and broke the mould of Thai politics. Thaksin didn't talk down to ordinary people and made the effort to formulate and implement policies that directly benefited them. They loved him for it, and re-elected him with a massive majority in 2005. James Stent observes that Thaksin's approach to politics changed Thailand forever:

> Thaksin astutely recognized that the majority of voters were resident in the countryside, and that they had, over the preceding decades of steady economic development, become a sleeping but nonetheless restless giant that was just waiting to be awakened. Once awakened, that rural electorate has not returned to sleep. (Stent, 2010)

By 2006, as Bhumibol marked sixty years on the throne, bitter political conflict had erupted between Thaksin and Thailand's traditional establishment. Just three months after the Diamond Jubilee festivities, the army overthrew Thaksin with the overwhelming support of the elite and the acquiescence of the king. The myth that during his reign Bhumibol had overseen a steady evolution from military dictatorship to sustainable democracy unravelled – suddenly it seemed that instead of making progress, Thailand had just being going round and round in circles.

Contemptuous and dismissive of rural voters they regarded as uneducated, the establishment assumed the poor would meekly accept the coup and soon forget about Thaksin. They were wrong. By the twenty-first century, Thai villagers were no longer the obedient serfs the elite believed them to be:

> The confined world of rural Thai villages … in the 1950s, where spirits and officials were to be appeased and a traditional subsistence way of life was passed on from generation to generation

with little change, has radically changed. Now villagers are plugged into the rest of the world via television, mobile phones, pick-up trucks, and family members spending time working at wage earning jobs in Bangkok. As many taxi drivers, all hailing from countryside villages in the Northeast of Thailand, have told me, 'We really aren't as stupid as the city people think we are. We used to be stupid, but no longer.' (Stent, 2010)

Rural voters in the north and north-east were shocked by Thaksin's downfall, and widely expected Bhumibol to step in to restore democracy and uphold their rights, as they believed he had done in past political crises. When it became clear that the royalist establishment supported the coup, their bewilderment turned into disillusionment and anger. As Streckfuss argues,

> The coup and its aftermath caused an ideological implosion that threatens to rather unceremoniously shove Thai history out of its half-century old suspension and, perhaps, lead to its reckoning....
> Thai history no longer made any sense. Or maybe better said, the illusion of a progressive, democratic movement evaporated, revealing ... a core authoritarian mindset amongst the elite and intellectuals, part and parcel of a shared project to keep Thai society and history in suspension, and subject to systematic social injustice...
> The majority of people in Thailand, who live on the other side of this political divide, have become incredulous and enraged... Tempers seethed in the North and Northeast, as it seemed that everything was being done to thwart the will of the majority. Sovereignty, apparently, was not to be with 'the people'. (Streckfuss, 2011)

In the years that followed, it became increasingly obvious that, far from acting as a unifying institution above partisan politics, the palace was intimately involved in the unfolding conflict. Millions of rural and urban poor began to realize that the stories they had been told were lies. They resolved to educate themselves about the truth, with the help of community radio stations which became increasingly bold in challenging official ideology. Meanwhile, a growing number of progressive urban middle-class Thais also began questioning their assumptions about the monarchy. They were a minority of the mostly royalist Bangkok bourgeoisie, but they included many of the best and the brightest – particularly younger Thais who chafed at the rote learning and lack of curiosity inculcated by the country's notoriously atrocious education system and yearned for greater freedom and openness. Before the twenty-first century, Thais with doubts about the claims of ubiquitous royalist propaganda tended to feel isolated and alone, afraid to share their views in a society that widely viewed them as heretical. But the explosion of social media use among Internet-savvy younger Thais enabled like-minded people to communicate in relative safety for the first time. Hundreds of thousands created Facebook profiles using fake names to protect themselves from *lèse-majesté* charges, and began swapping information and insights in online communities. When Bhumibol failed to intervene to halt the bloodshed in 2010, it was the final straw for millions of Thais, particularly the Red Shirts and their sympathizers. As the military closed in on the protest encampment at Ratchaprasong during May 2010 and the death toll rose, a banner hanging from an overpass plaintively asked: 'Where's Dad?'

Anti-monarchist sentiment had been growing exponentially since 2006, but when it exploded into the open on 19 September 2010 it was a breathtaking breach of the taboo on insulting the monarchy, and a spectacular breakdown of the social norms of obedience and deference to authority that the state has long tried to inculcate in Thailand's people. It rocked the traditional hierarchical cosmos of Thai society and appalled the kingdom's elite. 'The historical importance of this day cannot be underestimated, especially the organic manner in which all this occurred, without any organization at all, no leaders', said journalist Nick Nostitz, who covered the protest that day. He described it as an 'ideological bomb' that 'has brought fear into the hearts of the elites and the military' (Nostitz, 2011b). What made the incident so threatening to Thailand's establishment was not only the unprecedented defiance and audacity of the protesters. Even more worryingly, it showed that the royalist myths and fables that had underpinned Thailand's unequal and exploitative social and political structure for centuries were losing their magic.

As this unprecedented challenge to his moral authority unfolded, Bhumibol was about four miles away, in a sixteenth-floor suite in Siriraj Hospital on the west bank of the Chao Phraya river. He had been admitted to the hospital a year before, and had been resident there ever since, unwilling or unable to leave, even when doctors pronounced him fit to be discharged. In a radio broadcast in August 2010 to mark her birthday, Sirikit insisted her husband was doing fine: 'Now his health has substantially improved but doctors still ask him to continue doing physical therapy so that he can move around with strength first before leaving the hospital' (Vithoon, 2010). It wasn't true. Doctors had cleared Bhumibol to go home back in October 2009. At any of his palaces he could receive the best medical care money could buy. The truth was that he was refusing to leave Siriraj. He seemed to be trying to escape the burden of being king.

Bhumibol had been a lonely, socially isolated figure throughout his reign. As maverick royalist Sulak Sivaraksa told US magazine *Fellowship* in a 1992 interview:

He's a very nice man, but he has no friends, and he knows it.
People surround him, flatter him, and so on. In Buddhism, the
concept of a good friend is very important. And a good friend is
someone who is willing to tell you the truth, willing to criticize
you, telling you your weaknesses. As human beings, we all have
weaknesses. And sometimes we know, sometimes we don't... And
unfortunately, either with kingship or presidency or whatever,
when you are so high up, people flatter you. And they flatter you so
often, you believe them. (Sulak, 1992)

Elder statesman Anand Panyarachun, a member of the king's
inner circle, told US ambassador Boyce in 2007 that he was
worried about the effect of this environment on Bhumibol's
mental health:

Anand said he was less concerned about the King's physical health
than about his ability to receive objective advice and to benefit
from the company of friends. Anand remarked that half the people
who work at the Palace did so only to acquire status and peddle
influence; only around one-third of those at the court were there
solely out of devotion to the King. He said the King was lonely and,
for the most part, could not select the people with whom he spends
his time. (07BANGKOK940)

In late 2009, as Bhumibol's hospital stay inexplicably length-
ened, several contacts of the US embassy, including Suthep
Thaugsuban, deputy leader of the ruling Democrat Party, told
diplomats they believed the king was sunk in severe depression:
'Tapping his forehead, Suthep claimed that the King's physical
health was okay, but that the ... worry was his state of mind,
depressed at the state of affairs in his Kingdom at the end of his
life' (09BANGKOK2606).

Isolated in hospital, decrepit and possibly paralysed by depression, Bhumibol seemed to have abandoned any active role in
seeking a solution to Thailand's crisis. As he faded, the authority

of the monarchy faded too. The bonds holding Thailand's traditional hierarchical society together were fracturing and decaying.
On rare occasions the king would attend a ceremony or engagement somewhere in the city, but he always came back to his room
in the hospital. Sometimes he was taken down to the hospital pier
beside the river for brief appearances, in a wheelchair and usually
accompanied by his favourite dog, Tongdaeng. On 29 September,
the king was wheeled to another part of the hospital, dressed in
a tuxedo and black bow-tie, for a musical recital in his honour.
A frail, shrunken Bhumibol, his neatly combed and side-parted
hair streaked through with grey, sat impassively as the Thailand
Philharmonic Orchestra played the jazz tunes he had composed
many years before, as a young man, in love with Sirikit: *Blue Day,
No Moon, I Never Dream, Love at Sundown, Falling Rain, H.M.
Blues*. The concert organizers said the date was chosen because it
was thirty-four years since the last time the king had played music
in front of a student audience. He used to do this regularly, but
stopped after 29 September 1976. Nobody mentioned why – the
massacre of students at Thammasat a week later that tore apart
any pretence of Thai harmony, and the dark, paranoid, divided
years that followed. The king had emerged from that crisis and
rebuilt his reputation, but as Thailand tumbled deeper into conflict once again he seemed bewildered and helpless. Bhumibol had
become a spectral figure, his authority and vitality dimming, as
Thailand unravelled around him.

Long before, during his sea voyage from Europe back to Thailand aboard the diesel liner *Selandia* for his coronation ceremony
in 1950 with his fiancé Sirikit, the 22-year-old King Rama IX
had received some advice from his future father-in-law Prince
Nakkhatra Mangala, who was also aboard the ship. Years later,

during a conversation with his biographer William Stevenson in the 1990s, Bhumibol recalled that the prince had explained that royal ritual and tradition were immensely important. 'When the legends die, all collapses', Nakkhatra warned him. 'Angkor Wat was the centre of a great empire and now it's overrun by monkeys' (Stevenson, 1999).

The evening of 19 September 2010 was the moment it became clear that the legends of Thailand's ruling class were dying. Bhumibol's kingdom was in crisis.

TWO

'In a never-never land, never mind'
Welcome to the Land of Smiles

Thais are taught from their earliest childhood that Bhumibol is a preternaturally talented and wise monarch who has single-handedly brought progress and development to the nation through more than six decades of heroic effort. This is the story told by daily royal news broadcasts, school textbooks, official histories, newspapers and propaganda films. In classrooms throughout Thailand, with a photograph of their monarch invariably gazing benevolently down from the wall, schoolchildren are told that throughout their history it has always been their kings who have provided the Thai people with everything they have reason to be grateful for. As a textbook for primary school children explains,

> From time immemorial, the Thai kings have loved and been worried about the populace, as a father about his children. As a leader, the king has promoted the good and prosperity of the country so that the populace could always enjoy peace and happiness. That is why we worship the institution of king forever. (Educational Technique Bureau, 1978)

In her impassioned essay 'Why I Don't Love the King', labour activist Junya 'Lek' Yimprasert describes how adoration of Bhumibol and Sirikit was ingrained in her as she grew up in a rural community:

Old pictures of the young and beautiful King and Queen, and of
the prince and princesses, were always on the empty wall of our
family's house. No matter how many times we had to build or
rebuild our home, these pictures were always with us, and always
returned to the highest spot of the wall. They were still there on
the empty wall when I last visited my home, colours faded and
stained at the corners by raindrops.

As soon as I could open my eyes I saw the picture of the King,
as soon as I could understand a few words I was told that we must
love the King and Queen because they are our King and Queen.

We were made to believe they are the greatest of all Kings and
Queens, and in those days TV was saturated with programmes
about royal projects and charities to prove it. No one in my family
had ever met the King, but we all loved the King because everyone
said he is a good King.

When I was very small we used to go to the neighbours to watch
TV. My grandmother and mother were addicted to the regular 8
p.m. news about the Royal Family. Making sure they watched the
royal news was part of their code of practice for being a proper
citizen. When the Government said light a candle for the King they
did so without question, and they really did love the handsome
King and the beautiful Queen, the young prince and the princesses,
and never stopped commenting on how graceful they looked...

This is how I loved my village and how we 'loved' the King and
Queen, long before I was able to think about the meaning of love.
(Junya, 2010)

Reverence for the modern monarchy draws on traditional
beliefs which still have remarkable potency in Thailand today.
The theology of Thai kingship comprises three intermingled
spiritual strands. First, primordial animistic beliefs remain very
much alive. For many Thais, magic is real and the world is full of
spirits who need to be appeased and respected. In this tradition,
the monarchy possesses particular magical powers and plays a
crucial role in ensuring harmony and order not only in society
but also in the natural world. These beliefs have been overlaid
by two of the world's great religions, both of which swept into

Southeast Asia from India – Hinduism and Buddhism. In Hindu kingship, adopted by the Thais from the Khmer empire based at Angkor, which flourished from around the ninth to the fifteenth centuries, the monarch is semi-divine, a living god or *devaraja*, whose legitimacy derives from his sacred blood. In Buddhism – the religion most Thais follow today – the king is a *dhammaraja* whose legitimacy is based on his great spiritual merit. There is an inherent contradiction between these two paradigms – in Hinduism the king is born great, while in Buddhism the king must achieve greatness through meritorious behaviour. Belief in karma and rebirth was what resolved the contradiction and allowed the ideologies to coexist. Being born into royalty was regarded as a result of achieving great wisdom and merit in previous incarnations. A monarch's royal blood was proof of the purity of his soul.

But the modern ideology of Thai royalism that underpins the political and social structure of the state is not some quaint cultural holdover from the distant past. In the twentieth century, as monarchy after monarchy toppled around the world and a bloodless revolution in Siam stripped the king of absolute power, the palace and its supporters set out to revive and reinvent royalism to safeguard their continued relevance and power. As Benedict Anderson has observed, '"Royalism" in the sense of an active quest for real power in the political system by the royal family ... persists in a curiously antique form in contemporary Siam' (Anderson, 1978). A famous lecture by Prince Dhani Nivat in 1946, with Bhumibol in the audience, was a key moment in this process of reimagining royalty. Dhani quoted the anthropologist Bronislaw Malinowski:

> A society which makes its tradition sacred has gained by it an inestimable advantage of power and permanence. Such beliefs and

practices, therefore, which put a halo of sanctity round tradition and a supernatural stamp upon it, will have a 'survival value' for the type of civilization in which they have been evolved. ... They were bought at an extravagant price, and are to be maintained at any cost. (Malinowski, 1925)

This passage had an immense impact on Thai royalists in the twentieth century. H.G. Quaritch Wales, a British scholar who served as an adviser to kings Rama VI and VII in the 1920s, was heavily influenced by Malinowski (Quaritch Wales, 1931), and Bhumibol told his biographer William Stevenson that the words 'made a deep impression' on him (Stevenson, 1999). Thailand's royalists made a very deliberate and systematic effort to construct a halo of sanctity around a social order in which they would be firmly in charge.

An imagined historical narrative was created that portrayed the palace as crucial to Thailand's success and harmony. This was nothing new – history is generally written by the victors, and, because official chronicles had been overseen by the palace for centuries, the royals had long been able to present the version of events that suited them best. B.J. Terwiel has compared Siamese and Burmese chronicles to identify several episodes in which official Thai history was edited to remove inconvenient details such as military defeats, revolts and periods of vassalage to rival states (Terwiel, 2011). Members of the royal family and their inner circle have put immense effort into shaping how history is written – the latest example is the semi-official biography *King Bhumibol Adulyadej: A Life's Work*, published in 2011 (Grossman and Faulder, 2011).

In the official narrative, Thai history progresses in a linear narrative through three phases: the kingdom of Sukhothai, which lasted from around 1250 to 1350; the kingdom of Ayutthaya from around 1351 to 1767; and then, after a hiatus rarely discussed in detail, the Bangkok era of 1782 to the present day. To support claims that from the earliest days of Thai history the monarchy was benevolent and progressive, royalists rely heavily on an inscription on a stone pillar, apparently dating from 1292 and written in a strange script not found anywhere else, which describes the Suk-hothai kingdom ruled by King Ramkhamhaeng as a utopian realm where the people are happy and prosperous, and any problems can be quickly resolved by ringing a bell outside the palace:

> In the time of King Ramkhamhaeng this land of Sukhothai is thriving. There is fish in the water and rice in the fields. The lord of the realm does not levy toll on his subjects for travelling the roads; they lead their cattle to trade or ride their horses to sell; whoever wants to trade in elephants, does so; whoever wants to trade in horses, does so; whoever wants to trade in silver and gold, does so... He has hung a bell in the opening of the gate over there: if any commoner in the land has a grievance which sickens his belly and gripes his heart, and which he wants to make known to his ruler and lord, it is easy; he goes and strikes the bell which the king has hung there; King Ramkhamhaeng, the ruler of the kingdom, hears the call; he goes and questions the man, examines the case, and decides it justly for him. So the people of ... Sukhothai praise him. (Wyatt, 2003)

Extolling the virtues of the monarchy in a speech to the American Chamber of Commerce in 1974, the aristocratic Kukrit Pramoj quipped: 'You may have noticed that the last part is the first mention of a twenty-four hour service in human history' (Van Beek, 1983). In this bucolic paradise, the story goes, Thailand's people were happy and free – indeed, it is widely asserted that freedom has always been such a fundamental characteristic of the kingdom's people that the word 'Thai' literally means 'free'.

Another crucial element of royalist mythology is that thanks to the monarchy, Siam escaped colonization. According to the official story, King Mongkut and his son King Chulalongkorn – Rama IV and Rama V – cleverly played off the world's major powers against each other and demonstrated that Thais were just as civilized as the most advanced Western nations, thus ensuring the country remained free. 'Every Thai, regardless of their educational background, knows the first axiom of Thai history', notes Thongchai, 'that is, thanks to the great leadership of the Chakri monarchs, Siam was never colonized by the Westerners' (Thongchai, 2004).

During Bhumibol's reign, this reimagined history has been used as the basis for the construction of a royalist ideology that depicts the monarch as fatherly, democratic and sacred all at the same time. Prince Dhani stressed the paternal qualities of the king in ancient times: 'The monarch was of course the people's leader in battle; but he was also in peace-time their father whose advice was sought and expected in all matters and whose judgment was accepted by all' (Dhani, 1947). This notion has been reinforced by designating Bhumibol's birthday Father's Day in Thailand, while Sirikit's is Mother's Day. Thais are encouraged to feel a personal bond with the palace, as children of the 'Father of the Nation'. Constitutional scholar Borwornsak Uwanno claims that 'it should be no surprise that whenever problems occur in the country, be they floods, drought, hunger or political crises, Thai people would look up to their King, like children who are ill will look for their parents to be near and care for them' (Borwornsak, 2006).

'All of this means', observes Thongchai, 'that Thais who are currently sixty years old or younger grew up under the pervasive aura of an unprecedented royal cult' (Thongchai, 2008). Creation of this royal religion was by no means the work of the Thai establishment alone. The United States played a crucial role, funding domestic propaganda in Thailand and encouraging coverage from sympathetic American media to depict Bhumibol as a beloved, benevolent, modernizing monarch as an antidote to communism.

When Bhumibol became king in 1946, it was widely expected that the monarchy would soon fade into extinction. Amid rivalry between Britain and the USA over which would be the dominant power in Thailand in the post-World War II era, the American media were generally dismissive of Bhumibol at first, regarding him as symbolizing a bygone British-influenced era of fusty class-ridden tradition. After the young king returned from Europe in 1950 for his formal coronation, the cover of *Time*'s 3 April edition was a caricature of Bhumibol in full royal regalia and oversize spectacles, with the caption: 'In a never-never land, never mind'.

The Americans easily beat the British in the power struggle over Thailand, and quickly came to regard the country as crucial to their war against communism in the region. US media portrayals of Bhumibol became increasingly reverential. The next time Rama IX appeared on the cover of *Time*, in May 1966, it was a portrait of a steely Bhumibol in military uniform beside a smiling Sirikit with flowers in her hair, beneath the slogan: 'A MONARCHY FIGHTS FOR FREEDOM'. The accompanying article described Thailand's royal family as bravely fighting in the front line against the baleful spread of socialism:

> Seen on a soft spring night, the luminous spires of the Temple of the Emerald Buddha seem to float over Bangkok scarcely touched by the blare of traffic, the neon slashes of bars and the ragged hurly-burly of mainland Southeast Asia's largest city. So too does the Kingdom of Thailand, proud heir to virtually seven centuries

of uninterrupted independence, seem to soar above the roiling troubles of the region all around it.

Neighbouring Laos is half in Communist hands, Cambodia hapless host to the Viet Cong, Burma a xenophobic military backwater. The Chinese talons are less than 100 miles away, North Vietnam a bare twenty minutes as the US fighter-bombers fly from their Thai bases. Everywhere on the great peninsula, militant Communism, poverty, misery, illiteracy, misrule and a foundering sense of nationhood are the grim order of the Asian day.

With one important exception: the lush and smiling realm of Their Majesties King Bhumibol ... Adulyadej and Queen Sirikit, which spreads like a green meadow of stability, serenity and strength from Burma down to the Malaysian peninsula – the geopolitical heart of Southeast Asia. Once fabled Siam, rich in rice, elephants, teak and legend, Thailand (literally, Land of the Free) today crackles with a prosperity, a pride of purpose, and a commitment to the fight for freedom that is Peking's despair and Washington's delight. (McManus, 1966)

Paul Good, who worked for the US Information Service in Thailand from 1963 to 1968, has described US propaganda efforts during this period:

We had a program which had been instituted with the purpose of solidifying the Thais behind their king... We were in effect a PR unit for the Thai government. We would pass out pictures of the king...

The purpose was to show the people that the King was thinking of them and taking care of them and interested in listening to what they had to say, on the theory that if the people were supportive of the King, that he would be the binding force, the focal point for all attention, and there wouldn't be any susceptibility to the communist influence which was coming in on the Laotian and Cambodian sides from Vietnam. That was the theory. We pinned up a lot of pictures of the King, which were printed in our Manila printing plant. (Good, 2000)

Over the decades, thanks to the propaganda efforts of the USA, the Thai establishment's efforts to inculcate royalism, pliant local newspapers and a Western media that lapped up the fairy-tale narrative of an exotic land with a monarchy courageously combating communism, a now-familiar narrative emerged. Thailand was a haven of freedom and harmony in a troubled region, a country full of charming and obliging natives who lived carefree lives, all thanks to the immense hard work and unrivalled moral authority of the saintly saxophone-playing King Bhumibol.

An article by Pico Iyer in 1988, again in *Time* magazine, was typical. Iyer described Thailand as 'a travel agent's dream: first-class services at Third World prices, exoticism crossed with elegance', and dismissed the regular seizures of power by the country's military as irrelevant because the revered monarchy provided political stability: 'the land itself, for all its cyclone-cycle coups, is a pocket of relative calm and one of Washington's surest friends: the more the government changes, the more the monarchy stays the same.' Iyer dropped appreciative hints about the quality of the country's vast industrialized sex industry – 'postprandial appetites … are taken care of in a night world as treacherously bewitching as any on earth – one winking neon blur of bars and discos and imperial, four-story massage parlors' – and also commended the shopping, calling Bangkok the 'bargain basement of the East'. The role of royalty in this cut-price nirvana was evoked in glowing prose:

> Here is a never-never land built on solid ground; a fairy-tale monarchy ruled by a Renaissance King and his classically beautiful Queen; an orchid-scented garden of scintillant temples, lush jungles, palmy white beaches and a capital built along tree-shaded canals; and a gentle Buddhist retreat filled with smiling, gracious people who make 'tourist industry' sound like a contradiction in terms. The most pressing problem with the 'Land of Smiles' may be simply that it is too hard to resist. (Iyer, 1988)

In fact, the Land of Smiles has a bigger problem – it doesn't exist. The never-never land was built on thin air, not solid ground. Ruling classes in all countries try to invent traditions that legitimize their supremacy, and nationalist narratives that veer far from objective reality are by no means unique to Thailand. But even in this context, Thai official history is surprisingly fantastical. A critical examination of official ideology induces a dizzying sense of vertigo as it becomes clear that almost nothing is true at all.

Thailand's ruling class is engaged in a ceaseless effort not only to conjure up its legitimizing fairy tales, but also to defend this fantasy world against the perilous encroachment of reality. The myth of the Land of Smiles survives through oppression and coercion. A crucial element of royalist ideology is the notion of 'Thainess' – said to be a national trait that captures the essence of what it means to be Thai. Thainess encompasses a set of approved behaviours and beliefs revolving around respect for authority, deference to social superiors, and – of course – unquestioning love for the king. As David Streckfuss and Thanapol Eawsakul note: 'At least since the 1960s, there are literally no definitions of Thainess in which the monarchy is not its central focal point' (Streckfuss and Thanapol, 2009). Reverence of the monarchy is characterized as a defining element of Thai identity, with those questioning the central place of the palace in politics and society condemned as 'un-Thai'. Hard-core nationalists regularly ask aloud whether dissenters are really Thai, and suggest they leave the country if they don't like Thai ways.

Thainess is imposed on the population through indoctrination – schoolchildren are routinely expected to prostrate themselves before their teachers, for example – as well as social sanctions for those who break the accepted code of behaviour. But it is also enforced by strict legal sanctions against defamation, which remains a criminal offence, and above all by the *lèse-majesté* law. The law has never been enforced on a large scale – through most of Thailand's modern history there have only been a few convictions per year, often apparently arbitrary rather than focusing on serial offenders or obvious threats to the state. This is a deliberate strategy, which a confidential US cable characterized using the proverb: 'Kill the chicken to warn the monkey' (09BANGKOK2342). A few unlucky souls each year are sucked into a legal nightmare and usually jailed for years for trivial comments, and this instils fear in the wider population.

To give a few examples, popular singer Pensri Poomchusri and her husband Suwat Woradilok were charged in 1957 after a neighbour complained they had named their dogs Bhumibol and Sirikit. The case went all the way to the Supreme Court, which sentenced Suwat to five years in jail. In 1983, student Rattana Utthaphan was sentenced to six years in prison for writing a letter to Bhumibol – whom she revered – imploring him to abdicate so he could enter politics. Other absurd past cases were mentioned in a US cable quoting Thai lawyer Thongbai Thongpao:

> Esteemed lawyer Thongbai has significant historical perspective on the law, having represented numerous lese majeste defendants. In all of his many cases, he told us September 1, he has only managed to secure one acquittal, and that was primarily because of a legal technicality. In terms of the severity of sentencing, he cited many examples of four year sentences for what he considered trifling acts: a man was convicted for suggesting that it was not necessary to hang the photos of the King and Queen in a meeting room; a newspaper columnist was jailed for ending his column with the quote, 'In the land of the blind, the one-eyed man is King.' The crux of the matter for Thongbai is that the lese majeste sentencing is as inequitable as the application of the law generally. (09BANGKOK2342)

The establishment defends the law by claiming that Thailand's people demand it, as they love the king so much they cannot stand for him to be traduced. Streckfuss notes the weakness of this argument: 'The difficulty for defenders of the law is to explain how the institution of Thai monarchy could be so utterly loved if it required the most repressive lèse majesté law the modern world has known' (Streckfuss, 2011).

The oppressive influence of the elite weighs on discourse at all levels of society, silencing dissenting voices. As Andrew Turton observed in his studies of rural Thais, traditionally the poor 'have no voice':

> If they raise their voices to protest their conditions, or criticize some new official scheme which they perceive not to be to their advantage, they are not listened to, their voices have no weight… Or they feel the weight of dominant others' authoritative discourse so heavily that they will not speak at all.

'It is not that the poor have nothing to say, or do not want to say it', Turton adds, noting that in private they often explain their silence with the phrase: 'I thought of what I wanted to say but couldn't utter it' (Turton, 1984).

Several academics have noted the unusual importance of ensuring everything has a pleasant appearance in Thailand, regardless of the underlying reality. Peter Jackson refers to this phenomenon as 'the Thai regime of images' (Jackson, 2004a) while Rosalind Morris has described it as the Thai 'order of appearances' and 'the love of the disciplined surface' (Morris, 2000). The importance of preserving a positive image – or saving face – is widely considered a common Thai trait, and numerous cultural acclimatization guides for foreigners warn that 'breaking the face' of a Thai is a serious social transgression. Etiquette dictates that the country's people should remain silent about all the ways that reality falls short of the ideal, and inconvenient truths are to be politely ignored, never uttered. In a study of Thailand's sex industry, Ryan Bishop and Lillian S. Robinson describe the consequences:

> the unspeakable operates as social decorum and appropriateness, as well as reputation or face saver. In particular, and this may be partially due to decades of media censorship, most evocations of any issue that reflect negatively on the Thai nation are met with refutation or outright denial. Particularly taboo are the monarchy and the sex industry. Although Thais often gossip about both in small groups of intimates, these same people will deny the validity of such utterances in larger groups, especially those composed of their colleagues or people of higher social rank... The government strongly encourages such discursive deceptions: hence the perpetuation of cultural aphasia. (Bishop and Robinson, 1998)

In this environment, stating the obvious can have unexpectedly incendiary consequences. In May 2012, Lady Gaga flew into Bangkok for a sell-out concert and sent a cheery message to her 24 million Twitter followers: 'I just landed in Bangkok baby! Ready for 50,000 screaming Thai monsters. I wanna get lost in a lady market and buy a fake Rolex' (Lady Gaga, 2012). Fake luxury watches are some of the most popular tourist souvenirs from Bangkok, openly on sale in seedier parts of the city. But by mentioning an issue Thais prefer to leave unspoken, Gaga violated one of the country's unwritten rules. Thousands took to social media and online forums to denounce her. A protest rally was hastily organized, and the director general of Thailand's Department of Intellectual Property considered the issue serious enough to warrant a formal response, condemning Gaga's tweet as 'offensive, insulting and creating a bad image for the country' (Petchanet, 2012).

One of the most remarkable achievements of Thailand's establishment has been shutting down portrayals of the monarchy that they disagree with, even far beyond the country's legal jurisdiction. In 2002, an advertisement for Saint Jack's bar in Philadelphia, which ran twice in the local *City Paper*, caused a diplomatic storm because it depicted a 'bling bling' Bhumibol with gem-encrusted sunglasses, blond highlights and shaved tramlines in his hair, and an Adidas logo on his robes. 'I was basically taking elements from Thai culture and combining it with elements of hip-hop', the ad's designer, Steve Weiss, told the *City Paper* after the controversy erupted. The bar began receiving irate calls and abusive emails from Thailand. Voravee Wirasamban, Thailand's consul general in New York, wrote to bar manager Sherry Levin denouncing the ad as 'an affront to the Thai people' and demanding that the bar 'make a reparation for this uncouth ridicule at the expense of our beloved King'. His deputy, Boonsam Watanapanee, warned: 'Thousands and thousands of Thai will come to your place, to the restaurant... It wouldn't be nice.' Even the Thai ambassador to the United Nations got involved. Eventually, Saint Jack's decided to stop running the ad (Altman, 2002).

Unwilling to face this kind of intimidation, even media organizations with no staff in Thailand to protect have been reluctant to publish anything that might be construed as insulting to the monarchy. The Thai elite have succeeded in propagating the notion that any challenge to royalist fables is an act of grave cultural desecration, akin to blasphemy and unspeakably offensive to all Thais. No other country in the world, not even China – which rigorously polices foreign journalism within its borders and has far greater international influence – has been so successful at dissuading the rest of the world from challenging the myths of its ruling elite.

An important reason for the resilience of the official narrative is that it's such a beguiling story compared to the grim reality of contemporary Thailand. Many Thais cling particularly tightly to their belief in Bhumibol's virtue because throughout the kingdom's modern history there has been so little else for them to have faith in. Exploitation and corruption are entrenched at all levels of society. Ministerial positions are routinely held by mafia 'godfathers' or their wives, children and business cronies – usually incompetent at fulfilling their official duties but exceptionally adept at embezzlement and graft. Politicians, police, military officers, tycoons and criminals have colluded in looting the country with impunity. Organized crime networks have become intimately linked with, and often indistinguishable from, the Thai state. In the decades since World War II, Thai society has suffered corrosive upheaval and dislocation due to rapid urbanization, the cancerous growth of heroin and methamphetamine abuse, and the unrestrained expansion of the sex sector. In this blighted political and social landscape, Rama IX appeared to be the only beacon of hope. Despite all the reasons for disgust and despair, Bhumibol's perceived goodness allowed people to be proud to be Thai. The possibility that the Land of Smiles doesn't really exist is too awful to acknowledge. But most Thais know, at some level, that the fairy tales aren't true.

Such a stark disjunction between private beliefs and public behaviour and discourse is characteristic of totalitarian societies – putting on an outward show of loyalty and deference is all-important. As Jackson notes: 'the distinctiveness of Thai power lies in an intense concern to monitor and police surface effects, images, public behaviours, and representations combined with a relative disinterest in controlling the private domain of life' (Jackson, 2004a). There is a strikingly theatrical quality to Thai political and social interactions. The ruling elite use propaganda and enforced behavioural norms to conjure up a fairy-tale kingdom, and even Thais who find royalist fables ridiculous mostly pretend to believe in them and make the effort to behave accordingly. The famous Thai smile is a mask that can conceal any number of emotions. And so Thailand's people, however unwillingly, generally cooperate in acting out their designated roles in an epic performance directed by the elite. Heckling the show is outlawed. As an American businessman with royal connections despairingly observed in comments to the US ambassador, cited in a leaked cable: 'these people live in an alternate reality' (09BANGKOK325).

THREE

'Cosmological bluster'
The dramatics of despotism

If a member of Thailand's royal family has to be executed – a fate
that has befallen hundreds over the centuries, usually for trying to
seize the throne or after having the throne seized from them – the
killing has to be conducted in a very particular way. The method
was set out in the voluminous palace law promulgated by King
Trailok in 1456, which still governs the monarchy. Trailok's legal
code stipulated that errant royals should be put inside a velvet sack,
beaten to death with fragrant sandalwood clubs, and then flung
into a river. The executioner thus avoided breaking one of the most
important taboos of all – it was absolutely forbidden to spill royal
blood. The fact that a human being was being bludgeoned to death
was tastefully concealed by the velvet sack, and the appearance of
venerating royalty was – in theory, at least – preserved. As Quaritch
Wales observed in his study of Thai royal ritual:

> Such a peculiar method of reasoning is supported by the theory
> that blood is the vehicle of life, and to let the blood escape is the
> most obvious method of inviting death; which reminds one of the
> Siamese fisherman's excuse that he does not actually kill the fish,
> but merely takes them out of the water, after which they proceed to
> die of their own accord. (Quaritch Wales, 1931)

From the emergence of the first Thai kingdoms around a millennium ago, the elite have relied on ritual and theatrics to deny

reality. The depiction of medieval Siam as a harmonious realm ruled by fatherly monarchs is pure fantasy. The premodern Thai state was a ramshackle despotic machine designed to control its inhabitants and extract labour and tax from them. Quaritch Wales, who shared the view of the Siamese elite that absolute monarchy was the system best suited for the country's allegedly primitive people, nevertheless had no illusions about the nature of royal rule:

> In old Siam the inhabitants of the country were considered only as the goods and chattels of the king, who had absolute power over their lives and property, and could use them as best suited his purpose. Otherwise they were of no importance whatever...
>
> The absolutism of the monarch was accompanied and indeed maintained by the utmost severity, kings ... practising cruelties on their subjects for no other purpose than that of imbuing them with humility and meekness. Indeed, more gentle methods would have been looked upon as signs of weakness, since fear was the only attitude towards the throne which was understood, and tyranny the only means by which the government could be maintained. (Quaritch Wales, 1931)

The basic political units in premodern Southeast Asia were constellations of settlements revolving around fortified towns, surrounded by wilderness. The region was starkly underpopulated, and mostly covered by forest. Wet-rice cultivation was the dominant mode of agriculture, as it still is. Land was plentiful, but people were scarce, and the cycle of wet-rice cultivation required a few periods of labour-intensive activity each year, interspersed with longer idle spells. The political and economic structure of communities was shaped by the requirements of food production, and particularly irrigation – leaders needed to control the supply of water, and they needed to control manpower. To entrench their dominance, force alone was not enough, because unhappy

Premodern resistance to the state: the Zomia hypothesis

In his acclaimed book *The Art of Not Being Governed*, anarchist scholar James C. Scott argues that hill communities in upland Southeast Asia contain the descendants of people who had escaped state control, and that their whole culture evolved partly as a way of keeping efforts to govern them at bay: 'Hill peoples are best understood as runaway, fugitive communities who have, over the course of two millennia, been fleeing the oppressions of state-making projects in the valleys – slavery, conscription, taxes, corvée labor, epidemics, and warfare'. Scott draws on evidence from the social and economic structure of hill communities, and their culture and ideology, to support his thesis:

> Virtually everything about these people's livelihoods, social organizations, ideologies, and (more controversially) even their largely oral cultures, can be read as strategic positionings designed to keep the state at arm's length. Their physical dispersion in rugged terrain, their mobility, their cropping practices, their kinship structure, their pliable ethnic identities, and their devotion to prophetic, millenarian leaders effectively serve to avoid incorporation into states and to prevent states from springing up among them.

The hypothesis is based on studying a region he calls Zomia, which includes all the lands at altitudes above 300 metres stretching from the Central Highlands of Vietnam, through Laos, China, Thailand and Myanmar to north-eastern India, 'containing about one hundred million minority people of truly bewildering ethnic and linguistic variety'. Scott argues that Zomia is 'the largest remaining region of the world whose peoples have not yet been fully incorporated into nation-states'.

In a reversal of the conventional wisdom that hill tribes are primitive people who never developed a more sophisticated society, Scott argues that they chose to live this way after escaping oppressive lowland regimes, and developed their way of life partly to keep predatory states at bay. 'Civilizational discourses never entertain the possibility of people voluntarily going over to the barbarians, hence such statuses are stigmatized and ethnicized', writes Scott, noting that his 'account of the periphery is sharply at odds with the official story most civilizations tell about themselves':

> According to that tale, a backward, naïve, and perhaps barbaric people are gradually incorporated into an advanced, superior, and more prosperous society and culture. If, instead, many of these ungoverned barbarians had, at one time or another, elected, as a political choice, to take their distance from the state, a new element of political agency enters the picture. Many, perhaps most, inhabitants of the ungoverned margins are not remnants of an earlier social formation, left behind, or, as some lowland folk accounts in Southeast Asia have it, 'our living ancestors'... They are 'barbarians by design'. (Scott, 2009)

members of the community could choose to leave, on foot through the forest or by river or sea, in search of another – hopefully better governed – archipelago of settlements. Poorly led communities could collapse due to depopulation and famine as residents fled. The most basic and effective act of resistance for those unhappy with their leaders was simply walking away. As Neil Englehart observes,

> The most extreme non-cooperative strategy was flight: to abandon all patronage... The forests of Siam were sufficiently dense and the mountains sufficiently rugged that it would be virtually impossible to find people who did not want to be found. Further, there were almost no roads, only paths through the jungle easily and often obscured by treefalls. (Englehart, 2001)

To prevent catastrophic loss of manpower and maintain power, leaders were engaged in a constant quest for legitimacy. The

most obvious way to earn this was through competence and fairness – maximizing the productive capacity of the community and
minimizing social conflict. But families that wanted to preserve
their power over multiple generations had to find a way to cope
with the fundamental weakness of all systems of hereditary rule
– however impressive a leader may be, there can be no guarantee
that their descendants will govern equally effectively. Since brute
force and oppression could destroy a community, some kind of
legitimizing ideology was needed. The Khmer rulers at Angkor
legitimized themselves via the blood cult of the *devaraja* god-king
borrowed from Hinduism. But after Theravada Buddhism took
hold in the region from the thirteenth century, the competence of
leaders came to be assessed in terms of how well they appeared to
conform to the ideal of the *dhammaraja* ruler, whose legitimacy
is based on religious merit rather than sacred blood.

In both the *devaraja* and the *dhammaraja* traditions, power
was self-legitimizing. In the spiritual model of karma and rebirth,
good deeds are eventually rewarded and bad deeds punished, in
a future life if not in this one. Those who live virtuous lives and
accumulate wisdom are reincarnated higher up the ladder of existence, which spans all life from insects and worms at the bottom
to high-born males at the top. So a powerful man – even one who
owes his power to a mere accident of birth – is assumed to have
achieved this position thanks to karma from past incarnations.
In this model, there is no acknowledgement that power corrupts,
and that therefore constraints must be placed on rulers to prevent
them abusing their position. On the contrary, power is evidence
of virtue.

Ruling dynasties invested heavily in theatrical displays of
merit. As Scott says:

> The symbolic and ideological format for state-making was known
> and observed by ambitious local leaders with even the slightest
> pretense to wider power. State mimicry – what I have called
> cosmological bluster – was copied from the Chinese or Indic high
> forms, with rudimentary materials and in miniature, right down to
> the most petty village chiefs. (Scott, 2009)

The strictures of Buddhist kingship did not necessarily force
monarchs to behave better, but just made it important for them
pretend. 'Unfortunately ... history makes it quite clear that the
teachings of Buddhism were no more successful in restraining
despotic rulers in Siam than were those of other religions else-
where', observed Quaritch Wales, 'and it was always easy for
a tyrannical monarch to expiate a life of crime by forcing an
army of slaves to build a giant pagoda' (Quaritch Wales, 1931).
Ruling dynasties invented mythical histories to give themselves a
spurious aura of legitimacy and permanence – a phenomenon that
British historian Eric Hobsbawm, writing about European royal
myth-making, famously described as 'the invention of tradition':

> 'Invented tradition' is taken to mean a set of practices, normally
> governed by overtly or tacitly accepted rules and of a ritual or
> symbolic nature, which seek to inculcate certain values and norms
> of behaviour by repetition, which automatically implies continuity
> with the past. (Hobsbawm, 1986)

Patrick Jory calls this legitimizing strategy 'Great Lineage
history' in a Thai context, noting that Siamese rulers consistently
sought to link their dynasties to the kings of the *Jataka* tales –
fables of the past lives of the Buddha, in both human and animal
form – and to claim for themselves the same sacred legitimacy,
called *barami* in Thai (Jory, 2002).

By the thirteenth century, the Khmer empire was decaying and
several Siamese city states threw off their vassal status. Around

1238, the city of Sukhothai in the central Chao Phraya river plain proclaimed its independence. Other kingdoms to emerge included Chiang Mai to the north, and Phetchaburi to the south. Further south, a Muslim sultanate was founded at Patani. Meanwhile, a rival kingdom to Sukhothai in the central plains founded the city of Ayutthaya in 1351. The notion of a linear emergence of a recognizable Thai nation, from Sukhothai to Ayutthaya and then the modern Bangkok era, is a myth of royalist Thai historiography (Terwiel, 2011). In the official ideology of the modern Thai state, with its obsessive emphasis on unity and 'Thainess' linking all the nation's people in reverence for a single, universally recognized monarchy, the notion of competing centres of power is an anathema. But, in fact, several kingdoms coexisted. Premodern states lacked any clearly defined territorial boundaries, and there was no sense among the population that they belonged to a coherent nation until the nineteenth century. Instead, states were powerful cities with some degree of control over vassal towns and villages that sent an annual tribute, paid taxes to the palace and provided manpower when required. In some areas the influence of two or more states might overlap, with towns sending tributes to more than one monarch. Moreover, the amount of territory over which a state exerted influence was not static. It waxed and waned over time, depending on the efficiency and military power of the centre. O.W. Wolters has famously described premodern Southeast Asian kingdoms as *mandala* states:

> The map of earlier Southeast Asia which evolved from the
> prehistoric networks of small settlements and reveals itself in
> historical records was a patchwork of often overlapping *mandalas*
> or 'circles of kings'. In each of these mandalas, one king, identified
> with divine and 'universal' authority, claimed personal hegemony

over the other rulers in his mandala who in theory were his
obedient allies and vassals...

In practice, the *mandala* ... represented a particular and often
unstable political situation in a vaguely definable geographical area
without fixed boundaries and where smaller centres tended to look
in all directions for security. *Mandalas* would expand and contract
in concertina-like fashion. (Wolters, 1982)

By the end of the fourteenth century, Ayutthaya had established itself as one of the strongest states in mainland Southeast
Asia. Control of manpower was absolutely central to its success. A
highly stratified hierarchy was enforced via coercion and ideology.
Ordinary people were assigned to a social superior, or directly to
the king, and had to work in their service for six months of each
year, as soldiers in their armies, serfs in their fields or labourers
constructing the infrastructure of the state. Beneath them, at
the bottom of the social pyramid, were slaves. Fitting the classic
Weberian model of patrimonialism, people at all levels of the
system were controlled and employed by a specific person higher
up in the hierarchy, rather than an institution (Weber, 1962). The
system was a vast network of social control constructed from
hierarchical personal relationships of exploitation and subjuga-
tion. The myth that the word 'Thai' means 'free' is not merely a
linguistic fallacy (Ferrara, 2014), but also a glaring misrepresenta-
tion of the reality of life for Thais during the past millennium.

King Trailok's fifteenth-century palace law formalized Ayutthaya's hierarchical feudal relationships by introducing a ranking
system called *sakdina* which allocated a numerical score to every
person in the kingdom, defining what rung they occupied in
society. In theory, the scores indicated the amount of land each
person was permitted to own, although this was largely a no-
tional correspondence – real status derived from control of people,

not land. The crown prince had 100,000 *sakdina* points, other members of the royal family had up to 50,000 points, and various ranks of nobles had a score that ranged from 10,000 down to 400 points for the least powerful. Administrative officials had between 50 and 400 points, artisans 50, ordinary people 25, and slaves just 5 points. Unmarried peasant women were deemed lowlier than slaves, with no points at all.

The law also enforced multiple taboos intended to enhance fear and awe of the monarch. It was forbidden to even look directly at the king – in his presence, one had to be prostrated on the ground, eyes averted. The theatrical splendour of royalty was reinforced by forcing people to see it only in snatched glances, underscoring the vast gulf in status. The exceptions were two occasions per year in which the king led a procession to reinforce the myth of his mystical control over water, watched by thousands of his subjects. Inside the palace too, among those with sufficient social status to be allowed through the gates, ritual and ceremony were used to heighten the impression of the king's magnificence. The monarch had to be addressed in a special court language, called *rajasap*, and his name was too sacred to be uttered by ordinary people. Blood-curdling punishments were inflicted on those who transgressed. W.A.R. Wood, Britain's consul in Chiang Mai in the 1920s, lists some of them in his *History of Siam*:

> For immoral intercourse with a lady of the Palace: the man to be tortured for three days and then killed: the woman to be killed.
> For introducing amatory poems into the palace: death.
> For shaking the king's boat: death.
> For a palace official who permits stray animals to come to the palace: death. The sentry on duty at the time to have his eyes put out.
> For kicking the door of the palace: the offender's foot to be cut off.

For striking the King's elephants or horses: the hand to be cut off.
For abusing them: the mouth of the offender to be cut.
For whispering during a royal audience: death. (Wood, 1926)

By the end of the sixteenth century, Ayutthaya had achieved unprecedented wealth and power in Southeast Asia. Thousands of foreigners, mainly traders and soldiers, began to settle in the capital. They described it as a splendid city, criss-crossed by canals in which lurked fearsome crocodiles, and noted the theatrical pomp and cruelty employed by the elite to keep the population submissive. Clifford Geertz famously coined the term 'the theatre state' to describe pre-colonial Bali in the nineteenth century, arguing that ritual and ceremony were an end in themselves (Geertz, 1980). Throughout its existence the kingdom of Ayutthaya also used lavish ceremonies – and ostentatious violence – to underscore the sacred power and dominance of the monarch.

Jacques de Coutre, a merchant from Bruges, arrived in Siam in 1595 and spent eight months there during the reign of King Naresuan. He described a royal procession in detail:

> When the king goes forth, he does so with great pomp and accompanied by all his guards in two rows. He goes quite naked, apart from a small piece of cloth covering his secret parts, but with no other robe. On his head he wears a mitre like a bishop's, fluted at the top and all in gold, and inserted with numerous precious stones and other jewels. Seated on an elephant with two golden hooks in his hands, he guides the beast... Around them marches all the trumpets, the horn players and drummers... Four huge umbrellas, signs of royal rank, were carried. Everything took place in total silence and we met no one in the streets... People were warned when he left his palace and by which roads he would pass. At that moment, one met not a soul, not even a dog. Not even barking was heard, for the dog and its owner would have been killed in the cruellest fashion on earth. (Smithies, 1995)

Coutre also attended a royal audience with Naresuan, and says the Ayutthayan monarch was seated on a throne more than 3 metres high, with two tigers chained to its base. His account of his time spent in Ayutthaya contains extensive discussion of arbitrary violence, including a description of the fate of an 8-year-old girl in the service of the queen who was accused of stealing a small piece of gold. She was executed along with twenty-seven others, who were judged guilty of not revealing her crime. Coutre witnessed their torture:

> They had one of their eyes removed; then the skin from their hands was detached and their nails were torn out. After a certain time, a piece of their flesh was cut from their backs and stuffed in their mouths. So that they should suffer slowly, they were roasted over a low fire, each in her own pan, until they died. (Van Der Cruyyse, 2002)

The ritualistic splendour of Thai kings and their tendency for sudden eruptions of murderous violence are themes of the long poem *Khun Chang Khun Phaen*, which was performed by troubadours during the Ayutthayan era and passed down orally from generation to generation. As Chris Baker observes, the poem's depiction of the monarchy is one of very few surviving indications of what ordinary Thais thought of their kings:

> In the poem, the king is a threat to life, liberty, rank, property and family. Although he is also a giver of these things, particularly to those who bring him victory in war, this aspect receives much less emphasis than his capacity to deprive. All the major characters, and many of the minor ones, lose life, liberty, property, rank, spouse or kin at the hands of the king.

Baker notes that at least once in each chapter, the king is introduced 'with a formal invocation similar to those in other literary works', in which he is presented as a resplendent figure 'surrounded by things of supreme beauty appropriate to the supreme merit which qualifies him as king'. But he also regularly appears as a tyrant ordering violence. In one passage he reacts with fury when his orders are misinterpreted during a buffalo hunt:

> The king was inflamed with rage, as if the Prince of Hell had blown a wind across his heart. He bellowed like a thunderclap...
> Hey, hey! Bring the executioners immediately... Off with his head! Stick it up on a pole and raise it high! Seize his property and all his people, right now!

At other points in the story, the king orders characters to be impaled in a forest, cut open with an axe, and declares that the inhabitants of Chiang Mai should be exterminated: 'Wherever they're found, slash them to dust, until their city is deserted and laid waste' (Baker, 2008).

Ayutthaya itself was laid waste in 1767 by invading Burmese armies which breached the city walls after a fourteen-month siege and sacked the Thai capital. The Burmese monarchy wanted to obliterate forever the rival empire to the east. But out of the ashes of the old kingdom a new one was built, still based on authoritarian control. A former general known as Taksin declared himself king and rebuilt a centralized state based in Thonburi, 40 miles downriver from Ayutthaya. In 1782, Taksin was deposed and executed by one of his generals. The usurper moved the capital across the river to the east bank, beside a small trading settlement. Consciously modelling the new city on Ayutthaya, he gave it an elaborately aggrandizing name: 'The City of Angels, Great City, the Residence of the Emerald Buddha, Capital of the World Endowed with Nine Precious Gems, the Happy City Abounding in Great Royal Palaces which Resemble the Heavenly

Abode Wherein Dwell the Reincarnated Gods, A City Given by Indra and Built by Vishnukarn'. It is more commonly known as Bangkok, capital of the Chakri dynasty that still reigns today. Its founder is referred to as Rama I, the great-great-great grandfather of the current king.

The Bangkok monarchy was no less oppressive than Ayut-thaya. The state still depended on corvée labour and slavery. The *sakdina* system was retained and expanded. In legal cases, the weight given to each person's testimony was declared to be in direct proportion to their *sakdina* points, a legalistic way of ensuring justice always favoured the strong against the weak. To control manpower, the state employed the practice of tattooing male commoners on the wrist with numbers or symbols to show who they belonged to and what their duties were (Terwiel, 1979). The ideology and ritual of despotic royal rule remained intact.

But in the nineteenth century, the Thai elite's strategy of employing ostentatious pomp and cruelty to help maintain their dominance suddenly became perilously counterproductive. The traditional Thai cosmos that revolved around the palace, with its rigid social hierarchy, patrimonial power structures, feudal economy and ideology of sacred royal authority, was shaken by the encroachment of an external threat even more perilous than the marauding armies of the Burmese and the Khmer. Thailand's ruling class found themselves besieged by the rapacious capitalist colonial powers of the West, and the dangerously subversive ideology they brought with them – democracy.

PART II

Thai-style democracy and its discontents

FOUR

'Our country belongs to the people – not to the king'
Thailand's unfinished revolution

On the morning of 24 June 1932, in the genteel seaside resort of Hua Hin, King Prajadhipok, Rama VII of Siam, was playing golf with his wife Queen Rambhai and two government ministers when they spotted a court official dashing towards them across the fairways. On the eighth hole of the royal course adjoining Prajadhipok's summer palace – a villa named Klai Kangwon, or 'Far from Worries' – the king learned that the monarchy faced extinction. A revolution was under way in Bangkok. Reformist bureaucrats and military officers had seized control of part of the capital, taking hostage most of the princes who ran the government. The usurpers issued a proclamation denouncing the royals as tyrants:

> The government of the king has treated the people as slaves and as animals. It has not considered them as human beings. Therefore, instead of helping the people, rather it farms on the backs of the people. It can be seen that from the taxes that are squeezed from the people, the king carries off many millions for personal use each year. As for the people, they have to sweat blood in order to find just a little money…
>
> You, all of the people, should know that our country belongs to the people – not to the king, as has been deceitfully claimed. (Pridi, 2000)

The little group of revolutionaries who had improbably seized the state were in an extraordinarily weak position. They had control of a few important buildings and about forty hostages, and were protected only by some armoured vehicles and a few hundred soldiers of tenuous loyalty. They had no hold over the rest of the country, or even the capital. Most soldiers who assembled outside the rebel headquarters before dawn had been lured there for a bogus military drill and knew nothing about any planned revolution. When one of the rebel leaders climbed onto a tank and proclaimed the end of the absolute monarchy, many troops were baffled but cheered the announcement anyway (Stowe, 1991).

The revolution was a staged illusion, another theatrical performance. 'The remarkable feature was that not more than seventy men in all were in the plot, yet it was so daringly conceived and so perfectly carried out, such that a hundred and fifty-year-old monarchy could face a spectacular fall within a few hours', royal historian Prince Chula Chakrabongse ruefully remarked (Chula, 1960). Throughout Thai history, conflicts have tended to be settled not by brute force, but by winning a symbolic victory through establishing superior legitimacy. Premodern warfare traditionally involved the leaders of opposing armies fighting a duel on elephant-back, rather than a fight to the death among the massed troops on each side. A seventeenth-century Persian account of Siamese warfare discussed its ritualistic nature:

> They have no intention of killing one another or inflicting any great slaughter because if a general gained a victory with a real conquest, he would be shedding his own blood, so to speak.
> The fixed custom is that when two factions have lined up before one another, a group from each side comes forward, beating kettle-drums and playing flutes, and the infantry and the horsemen

on both sides begin dancing and shouting and raising all the noise
they can. Every so often one army advances and the other retreats
and in that way the one that has some luck manages to catch the
other off guard. They rush up and surround their rivals and when
the victorious group like a pair of compasses draws a line around
the other army, the vanquished ... admit defeat and place their will
in the circle of obedience. (O'Kane, 1972)

Political conflict in Thailand over the past century has had
a similarly theatrical character – confrontations tend to be legitimacy contests rather than straightforward battles in which the
stronger side prevails. The advantage the rebels of 1932 had on
their side was a legitimizing ideology potent enough to intimidate
the royalist establishment and obscure the reality that they had
only established a tenuous hold over a few buildings, and had
needed stealth tactics and trickery even to do that. According to
the theology of Thai kingship they were upstarts with no royal
blood and no credible claim to power. But they derived their
legitimacy from the rival values of an alien civilization which
rejected the moral authority of hereditary monarchs. Thai royalism was facing an existential challenge from the completely
contradictory concept of democracy.

The Western powers that began greedily circling Siam in the
nineteenth century posed a dual threat to the dominance of the
elite. Most obvious was the danger that Siam would be annexed,
the monarchy removed, and a colonial administration installed.
But westerners also brought with them ideologies antithetical to
the theology that legitimized royal rule in Siam. 'Colonialism was
not only a political and economic project, but also a cultural and
intellectual one that had induced drastic changes in local cultures
across the globe', observes Thongchai (2000). Although they were
hardly very democratic themselves, and denied democracy to

their colonies, Western powers portrayed themselves as bringing 'civilized' values of democracy to the despotic cultures of the East.

The values of democracy were incompatible with the ideology of sacred kingship that had underpinned Siam's power structure for centuries. To deal with this dilemma, the elite became flexible in their use of theatrics, depending on whether they were playing to a domestic or Western audience. They presented a 'civilized' and 'modern' appearance for Western consumption while still employing the ritual and symbolism of kingship to maintain their dominance over the domestic population. As Jackson argues,

> This history produced a janus-faced regime that intensified its power over the local population in order to orchestrate national performances of 'civilized' behaviour for foreign consumption, which in turn enhanced the international status and helped secure the autonomy of Siam's ruling elites from direct Western political control. The implicit message that Siam's elites sought to convey to the Western powers through this mobilization of the population in the collective performance of civilization was something like 'You Westerners do not need to colonise Siam in order to make us civilised. We Thais are disciplined enough to subject ourselves to your standards of civilization.' (Jackson, 2004b)

The elite adapted their clothing and behaviour to suit different audiences, as Maurizio Peleggi observes:

> Western-style clothes were integrated into a hybrid ensemble signifying the Siamese elite's connection to a foreign civilisation that was instrumental to the definition of their own identity and yet distinct. As a result, different modes of self-presentation – one for the colonial stage, one for the domestic stage, one for the private realm – came into play, allowing for the negotiation of external expectations and personal tastes. (Peleggi, 2002)

The ruling class also concocted the myth that far from being an alien concept, democracy had always been integral to their governance. In 1833, Prince Mongkut – a son of Rama II with ambitions to become monarch himself – claimed he had found a stone obelisk inscribed with mysterious writing in the ruins of Sukhothai. Mongkut became Rama IV in 1851, and presented an alleged translation of the strange script to Britain's governor of Hong Kong, John Bowring, during negotiations on a free-trade treaty in 1855. This was the renowned Ramkhamhaeng inscription, which portrayed Sukhothai as a proto-democracy in which citizens could ring a bell to alert the monarch to their problems. Modern scholars overwhelmingly regard the inscription as fake, written by Mongkut to create the impression that Siam had always been democratic and persuade the British not to remove the monarchy (Chamberlain, 1991; Wright, 1995). Famously, Mongkut also hired an Anglo-Indian governess, Anna Leonowens, to educate his many children and help them become 'civilized' too.

Contrary to official history, the elite never really resisted Western colonialism in the nineteenth century. They fought for Siam to be a semi-colony in which their domestic political dominance was maintained. Kasian Tejapira describes the country as becoming 'an indirectly colonised dynastic state' in which the monarchy and elite linked 'resources-rich Siam to the burgeoning global chain of commodity production as the British Empire's most important rice depot' (Kasian, 2001). In the conceptual vocabulary of premodern politics, Siam's elite were submitting to becoming 'vassal rulers' of the British. As Jackson observes, this was presented 'as a form of liberty, from the West, rather than as subjection to a new form of local tyranny':

> The royalist historical narrative of great kings saving the country obscures the fact that the Bangkok monarchy both profited and became stronger as direct results of Siam's capitulation to the West. The country's economy, legal system, and public culture were subordinated to Western norms, and the former Siamese

tributary states of Laos, Cambodia, and some northern Malay states were ceded to France and Britain, respectively. Nevertheless, in the aftermath of these undoubtedly disruptive transformations the Bangkok monarchy extended and cemented its power over the regions of the old Siamese empire that remained under its control. Because it profited financially from the treaties with the Western powers, the absolute monarchy acquired resources that permitted it to intensify its authority over the local population to a much greater degree than in the pre-colonial period. (Jackson, 2004b)

Mongkut's theatrics led directly to his death. In August 1868 he invited Thai and foreign dignitaries on a journey through mosquito-infested swamps to demonstrate his skill in predicting a solar eclipse and show that Siamese science was not so backward as westerners presumed. His prediction was a triumph, but the trip was a disaster – Mongkut caught malaria and died.

As the old king had wished, his favourite son Chulalongkorn succeeded him at the age of just 15. He was to be the last of Siam's medieval-style monarchs. During his reign he amassed 153 wives and concubines, and continued the practice of incest common to Thai kings over the centuries, taking four of his half-sisters, all daughters of Mongkut, as his queens. The persistence of royal incest demonstrated the resilience of the *devaraja* cult belief that royal legitimacy derived from purity of blood. Even within the royal family there was effectively a caste system, with those of purer blood having higher rank. Having children with women from outside the royal family diluted the status of the offspring. A king who wanted children of the highest royal rank had limited alternatives other than fathering them with half-sisters, aunts or cousins (Kemp, 1978).

Like the kings of Ayutthaya, Chulalongkorn's life was constrained by ritual and taboo. In 1880, one of his queens drowned when her royal barge capsized. The fifteenth-century palace law expressly forbade anyone touching members of the royal family even to save them if they fell into a river – the penalty was death plus extermination of the culprit's family. This rule theoretically remained in force, with the result that Chulalongkorn's queen 'was drowned in full view of numerous bystanders who dared not save her' (Quaritch Wales, 1931).

The king's polygamy and incestuous marriages, the persistence of archaic ritual and the continued prevalence of slavery were cited by interventionist British officials as proof of Siam's despotism and backwardness. The potential danger to the Chakri monarchy was vividly illustrated by the overthrow of King Thibaw, the last monarch of Mandalay, who acceded to the throne in 1878 largely thanks to the slaughter of dozens of other claimants orchestrated by his ambitious mother-in-law. The British exploited the perception that the Mandalay monarchy was uncivilized as a pretext to expand their colonial holdings. *The Times* described Thibaw as 'a profligate and brutal potentate, who is subject to violent fits of homicidal mania, in the rare intervals during which he is not hopelessly drunk' (*The Times*, 1879). In 1885, the British humiliatingly removed the terrified king and his family from the palace on bullock carts, sending them into exile in the port town of Ratnagiri in the far west of India. Thibaw died there in 1916, never seeing Mandalay again (Shah, 2012).

Chulalongkorn knew the same fate could befall him, and from the 1870s launched modernizing reforms intended to transform the economic and governance structure of the country – but without undermining Chakri rule. He visited British-ruled India and Singapore and Dutch-ruled Java to see how colonial authorities administered their territories and learn lessons applicable to

Siam. Chulalongkorn also strove to appear modern and progressive, trying to keep his subjects quiescent without offering them democracy. Upon officially coming of age in 1873, the king theatrically announced that prostrating to royalty would be abolished. In 1884, alarmed by the expansionist ambitions of Britain and France, he asked the advice of westernized princes on how Siam could avoid annexation. The following year, they submitted their response. Eiji Murashima has provided a summary:

> The present problem facing Siam is to maintain national independence and a stable government. To resolve this problem, Siam must be accepted and respected by the Western powers as a civilized nation. Hence there is no choice but to bring about a new government modeled after the Western pattern, or at least after Japan, the only country in the East following the European way. According to European belief, in order for a government to maintain justice it must be based on popular consensus. Cabinet ministers must be selected from the elected representatives of the people and must be responsible to all the people. No nation in Europe can believe that Siam maintains justice since everything is decided by the king. It would also be dangerous for Siam if it should happen that the throne becomes vacant. Therefore the following reforms should be carried out:
>
> 1. change the absolute monarchy to a constitutional monarchy,
> 2. establish a cabinet system or ministerial government,
> 3. distribute power to the heads of departments,
> 4. promulgate a law of royal succession,
> 5. change the payment system for the bureaucracy from the commission system to a salary system,
> 6. promote equality under the law,
> 7. reform the legal system on the Western model,
> 8. promote freedom of speech, and
> 9. establish a merit system for the bureaucracy.
>
> (Murashima, 1988)

Chulalongkorn refused to countenance constitutional monarchy, in a reply also summarized by Murashima:

He was not the same oppressive absolute monarch as those in European history and was not so short-sighted as a frog inside a coconut shell. Therefore, he was not an obstacle to the prosperity and security of the country... Any limitation or distribution of his power would not contribute to [his] reforms. On the contrary, there could only be a bad effect on them. Hence a parliament was no use in Siam because not only were there no suitable and able people to participate in it, but a parliament itself would hamper and corrupt the reforms. (Murashima, 1988)

Chulalongkorn began trying to build a professional army and bureaucracy, as well as a capitalist economy to replace the old *sakdina* system based on personal loyalties and patron–client relationships. Bonded labour and slavery were gradually phased out. Meanwhile, he sent his vast brood of sons to be educated in the West, to make them 'civilized' by foreign standards.

By his death in 1910, Chulalongkorn appeared to have radically transformed the country, with an absolutist state replacing the despotic structure of the past (Kullada, 2004). His reforms changed the composition of the establishment, with a professional officer class and a Western-educated civilian elite emerging. But authoritarian rule had not ended. As Duncan McCargo observes, 'Thai reform was at heart a means of preventing change, rather than a method of implementing change' (McCargo, 2001).

Chulalongkorn's successor Vajiravudh, King Rama VI, epitomized the cultural confusion of early-twentieth-century Siam. He had the mannerisms and education of an English gentleman, educated at the Royal Military Academy at Sandhurst and Oxford University. Yet he fought bitterly to defend the privileges of the absolute monarchy, permitting greater freedom of speech but refusing to allow any movement towards democracy. Seeking to forestall demands for popular sovereignty, Vajiravudh promoted a nationalist ideology based on the myth that monarchs had been notionally elected to lead the people, and that the palace was synonymous with the country. Taking the theatricality that had always characterized Thai kingship to its logical conclusion, he was a keen amateur actor and translated several of William Shakespeare's plays. In 1918, alarmed by the downfall of the Russian royal family a year earlier, he founded a toy city in northern Bangkok with a thousand miniature buildings including palaces, hospitals, hotels, banks and a fire station, plus parks, canals and flyovers. Vajiravudh declared it a practice ground to teach Thais about governance, staging theatrical performances of democratic politics there with faux elections and parliamentary debates. He played the role of an ordinary politician – 'Mr Rama' rather than King Rama VI. It was a ritual designed to give Vajiravudh the legitimacy of seeming modern without instituting any democratic reforms. Meanwhile, his lavish spending on traditional royal ceremonies nearly bankrupted the state, and an emergent elite cadre of Western-educated bureaucrats were growing increasingly dissatisfied with the system of absolute monarchy. Not content with administering Siam on behalf of the royal family, they wanted a role in governing the country too.

Vajiravudh died in 1925, and his younger brother Prajadhipok became Rama VII, inheriting a troubled kingdom. Prince Damrong, a senior royal, lamented: 'The authority of the sovereign had fallen much in respect and confidence, the treasury was on the verge of bankruptcy, and the government was corrupted and the services more or less in confusion' (Batson, 1974). By the 1930s, Prajadhipok was floundering, openly admitting he found it hard to cope with – or even comprehend – Siam's economic problems. 'I'm only a soldier. How can I understand such things as the gold standard?' he exclaimed to fellow royals in 1931 (Chula, 1960). Far from projecting the image of a sacred and supremely wise monarch, he gave the impression of being an inadequate man far out of his depth. The growing influence of Western-educated commoners who wanted a share of political power panicked the traditional elite, who believed their privileged world was about to come crashing down. An old prophecy that the Chakri monarchy would last only a century and a half fuelled an atmosphere of paranoia during the festivities in April 1932 for the 150th anniversary of the founding of the dynasty. Two months later, when the absolute monarchy was toppled by the coup of 24 June, the *New York Times* reported that the revolution 'coincided strangely with an ancient prophecy that has been woven into the folklore of the nation' (*New York Times*, 1932).

Prajadhipok eschewed many of the traditional trappings and superstitions of sacred kingship and presented himself as a modern statesman. The scene in Hua Hin on the morning of the revolution illustrated the impact of Western culture on Thailand's elite. Dressed like an English gentleman, Prajadhipok was playing golf. He had adopted Western sexual norms too – in contrast to the harems of his ancestors, Prajadhipok had one wife and no children. 'Far from Worries' was a European-style villa, and Hua Hin had been modelled on an English seaside resort. But none of this could disguise the fact the monarchy monopolized political power. Prajadhipok was an ineffectual figurehead, but his family controlled the country. Upon hearing the news that rebels had proclaimed the end of the absolute monarchy, the king appeared to regard it as inevitable. He turned to Queen Rambhai and said: 'So, as I told you.' Urging her to finish her round of golf, he departed to deal with the revolution.

Nobody was killed in the 1932 coup, but it was even more brutal than the sacking of Ayutthaya in terms of the damage it inflicted on the prestige of royalty. In 1767, the Burmese had destroyed the capital and killed or enslaved many of the elite, but the rebels of 1932 had challenged the very idea of absolute kingship itself, proclaiming that sovereignty lay with the people, not the palace. The group behind the revolution was an alliance of bureaucrats and military officers who called themselves the 'People's Party'. Most of them had formulated their views in Paris in the 1920s while studying there on government scholarships. Prajadhipok chose a strategy of feigned capitulation, masking a determined effort by the royalist elite to minimize the extent of real political change. At the heart of the strategy was pretending that the royal family was enthusiastically democratic and embraced the principles of the revolution. In a proclamation on 26 June, the king declared he had been planning similar reforms all along: 'As a matter of fact we have long contemplated the institution of a constitutional monarchy and what the People's Party have done is quite right and receives Our appreciation' (Ferrara, 2012). The rebels backed away from pursuing their revolution to its logical conclusion, concluding that a constitutional monarchy was sufficient achievement. Leading members of the old establishment were allowed to retain powerful positions. Only one senior royal, Paribatra, was deemed too bellicose to be allowed to remain in Siam, and was packed off to exile in Java.

The revolution was greeted with apparent indifference in the capital, as the *Bangkok Daily Mail* reported:

Bangkok awoke this morning to find that the greatest political sensation in its 150 years of existence had taken place quietly and without forewarning in the early hours before dawn... Except for scattering crowds in the neighbourhood of the Throne Hall and the Grand Palace, there was not the slightest sign of excitement… Police were on duty as usual. Courts functioned. Mail collections and deliveries were as usual… There was no hysteria, no bad feeling anywhere.

For the vast majority of the population, little had changed. The rebels declared in their provisional constitution that 'the highest power in the land belongs to all the people' but that a fully elected government would take up to a decade to arrive, to give time for the population to be educated. Even the most progressive members of the group, like lawyer Pridi Banomyong, had an elitist opinion of ordinary people's readiness for democracy, as Judith Stowe observes:

> As for all the high-sounding rhetoric about the people and their rights, Pridi clearly envisaged them in much the same way as did the monarchy. They were a concept to be invoked rather than individuals who could be expected to play any role in decision-making. Indeed, in advocating a lengthy period of political tutelage, Pridi was unwittingly echoing the views of royal advisors who had stated that the people were insufficiently educated or mature to cope with a more participatory form of government. (Stowe, 1991)

Meanwhile, the old royalist establishment launched a relentless effort to roll back reforms. Prajadhipok was heavily involved. 'He established the king's secret service and started an underground network to work against the Revolution', notes historian Nattapoll Chaiching. 'This network involved members of the royal family, secret agents, assassins, military officers, civil servants and journalists – all of them loyal to the old regime' (Natapoll, 2010). Royalist conservatives soon seized power from more progressive members of the People's Party, and when a draft of the permanent constitution was made public in November 1932, its preamble described the monarchy as 'the greatest power in the world' and 'an incarnation of God with widespread fame'. It was promulgated on 10 December in a ceremony that featured Prajadhipok seated on an elevated throne wearing his full royal regalia for the first time since his coronation. The event 'aroused little public interest', observes Stowe, and 'people had to be rounded up to cheer outside the Throne Hall' (Stowe, 1991).

Prajadhipok secretly ordered the execution of all the People's Party, to be carried out on the first anniversary of their revolution. According to Nattapoll, they 'would have been decapitated on treason charges if they had not realized the plot and staged a coup on 20 June, only four days before their heads were to be displayed on spikes at the courtyard in front of the Grand Palace' (Natapoll, 2010). After this reversal, the royalists launched a full-scale military offensive in October 1933. It was defeated after fierce fighting. Prajadhipok left for England in January 1934, on the pretext that he needed treatment for his eyesight. He rented a manor house south-west of London, where he lived the life of a wealthy country squire.

The self-exiled king threatened to resign several times during disputes with the government over reforms limiting royal powers and nationalizing palace wealth. Finally, on 2 March 1935, at the Siamese embassy in London, Prajadhipok abdicated, claiming in his final statement as king that he and the monarchy were the true guardians of democracy: 'I am willing to surrender my former powers in favour of the people generally, but I refuse to surrender to any particular individual or party so that power can be used in an autocratic way without the people having any voice.' As Federico Ferrara argues, it was just posturing: 'Faced with the inevitability of abdication, it is likely that the King merely sought to establish some basis to claim that the decision to abdicate was driven primarily by concerns for the country, as opposed to his unwillingness to accept a ceremonial role' (Ferrara, 2012).

Three journalists witnessed the historic – and underwhelming – event. 'Probably never in history was the abdication of a king announced with so little formality', said the *New York Times*:

> The King's dapper young secretary, wearing grey flannel trousers and a pullover sweater beneath his coat, received the newspaper men in his little studio, which was littered with official documents, books, typewriters and sporting guns. Two others of the royal household and one of the Scotland Yard detectives who are guarding the King were also present.
> 'Well, it's over now' said the secretary, standing before a roaring fire. 'He is no longer King.' (*New York Times*, 1935)

Prajadhipok never returned to Siam, dying in exile in 1941. But the old establishment never accepted that the era of absolute monarchy was over. They remained determined to subvert democracy and preserve rule by a royally anointed elite. It is a struggle still being fought today.

FIVE

'I really am an elected king'
The royalist revival

Bhumibol Adulyadej became King Rama IX of Siam in traumatic circumstances that seemed to herald the end of the political power of the Thai monarchy. On the morning of 9 June 1946, a gunshot rang out in the bedroom of his 20-year-old brother in the Grand Palace complex in Bangkok. A bullet had been fired into King Ananda Mahidol's forehead, exiting from the back of his skull. A clearly distraught Bhumibol was proclaimed Siam's new monarch later the same day. He was only 18 years old.

In the years following Prajadhipok's abdication, Thailand's old ruling class had seen their influence steadily eclipsed. Ananda was only 9 when he succeeded Prajadhipok as monarch, and was living in Switzerland with his widowed mother Sangwan Talapat, a commoner whose marriage to one of Chulalongkorn's sons had scandalized the royal establishment. He hardly even spoke any Thai, and his mother insisted he complete his education in Lausanne before formally taking up his royal duties. Meanwhile, the military faction of the 1932 revolutionaries, led by ambitious officer Phibun Songkram, became the dominant clique in Thai politics, marginalizing the progressives in Pridi Banomyong's circle and aggressively seeking to break the power of the royalists. Prominent princes continued their efforts to reverse the revolution and were responsible for several attempts to assassinate Phibun.

In November 1938 his valet fired a shot at him while he was dressing, and missed. A few weeks later, Phibun, his wife and several guests collapsed at a banquet and had to be rushed to hospital to have their stomachs pumped – the cook had poisoned the food. Phibun responded to royalist efforts to kill him by consolidating his power, forcing the prime minister to resign in December 1938 and taking the job himself. In early 1939 he ordered the arrest of fifty-one people, mostly princes, aristocrats and soldiers, on charges of treason, in another assault on the last vestiges of royal power. Styling himself as a nationalist leader in the mould of Mussolini, he changed the name of the country to Thailand, symbolizing a break with the old regime. The frail beginnings of democracy were being trampled, with absolute royal rule replaced by military dictatorship.

Thailand declared its neutrality when World War II began, but after France fell to invading German armies in 1940, Phibun saw the chance to bolster his nationalist credentials by seizing territory previously lost to French Indochina, with the acquiescence of the Japanese. Their help inevitably came at a price – in December 1941, Japanese forces invaded Thailand as part of their offensive to capture British-held Malaya and Singapore. Thailand was now a vassal state of Japan. Phibun proposed building a new capital in Phetchabun, which would symbolize the end of the Chakri era and the dawn of a new nationalist Thailand under Japanese tutelage. Meanwhile, Pridi secretly coordinated anti-Japanese resistance, aided by his old adversaries in the underground royalist network. Phibun was unexpectedly removed as prime minister in 1944, and then stripped of his command of the military. He was jailed after the US nuclear attacks on Japan ended the war in Asia in August 1945. Pridi Banomyong and his allies, who wanted to build a democratic Thailand, were finally in the ascendancy.

In December 1945, King Ananda returned from Switzerland. He was a shy and earnest youth. Louis Mountbatten, the commander of Allied forces in Southeast Asia, described him as 'a frightened, short-sighted boy, his sloping shoulders and thin chest behung with gorgeous diamond-studded decorations, altogether a pathetic and lonely figure' (Ziegler, 1985). US journalist John Stanton wrote:

> Ananda, Siamese remember, was a strange young King. Full of Western ideas, he refused to talk to visitors who sat on the floor below him in Siamese fashion, insisting that they sit on chairs level with himself. Since shyness is a Siamese characteristic, the visitors often found themselves unable to talk in such a presumptuous position; King and subject would sit in silence, both blushing. Siamese tell of Ananda's visits to little villages near Bangkok. He would summon up all his courage, walk up to an old woman and ask, 'Grandmother, how go things with you?' The woman would probably burst into tears at the thought that she had been addressed by a King, and Ananda would stand before her, eyes downcast and silent. (Stanton, 1950b)

Ananda seemed an ideal constitutional monarch for the new Thailand – a powerless but popular figurehead. Another constitution was promulgated in 1946, establishing a fully elected parliament for the first time. Pridi became prime minister, and Thailand appeared on the verge of sustainable democracy at last.

The mysterious shooting of Ananda shocked the nation. Initially, it was widely assumed that the young monarch had committed suicide. He had been shot with a Colt 45 pistol he kept by his bedside. The possibility that an assassin had somehow managed to get to the royal bedchamber, kill the king with his own gun, and escape without being seen seemed inconceivable. Sangwan, the grief-stricken mother of Ananda and Bhumibol, implored the government not to declare her son's death a suicide, and Pridi agreed to announce instead that Rama VIII had shot himself by mistake while handling his gun in bed. This was to prove a disastrous misjudgment. It was widely apparent that the official explanation was highly implausible. Desperate to regain their influence, the royalists began circulating rumours that Pridi had been behind the regicide as part of a communist plot. Meanwhile, the newly formed royalist Democrat Party began building an alliance of convenience with Phibun's military clique, also facing political extinction in the new Thailand. The traumatized and overwhelmed Bhumibol fled back to Switzerland with his mother, and seemed unwilling ever to return. But the mysterious shooting of Ananda continued to roil Thai politics, and the government was rendered dangerously vulnerable because of its failure to come up with a convincing account of what had happened.

In November 1947, the royalists and militarists made their move, overthrowing the elected government. The first major contribution of the Democrat Party to Thai politics was snuffing out the country's nascent democracy. They used widespread awareness that Pridi was hiding evidence about Ananda's death to legitimize their actions, and he fled Thailand in fear of his life. Bhumibol sent a message from Lausanne approving the coup. As historian Kobkua Suwannathat-Pian explains:

> The King's death profoundly affected contemporary Thai politics and politicians. The most outstanding victims of the fallout from the royal death were Pridi and his political supporters who were completely and effectively blotted out of Thai politics... The political demise of Pridi and the liberals and the ideals that they represented made it that much easier for the military and conservatives, each in turn, to mould the country's political system to their own tastes and requirements. (Kobkua, 2003)

Having crushed the progressives, the royalists and Phibun's military clique turned on each other. A constitution was drafted in 1947 that gave extraordinary powers to the monarch, and in 1948 a law was passed restoring control of royal wealth to the king. Phibun struck back by seizing power in April 1948, overthrowing the Democrat Party government and installing himself as prime minister once again. But he was unable to prevent the promulgation of a royalist constitution in 1949. As the two factions battled for supremacy, the reluctant Bhumibol briefly visited Thailand in 1950 to cremate his brother, marry Sirikit and formally crown himself king. He stayed only ten weeks before returning to Switzerland ostensibly to finish his studies, although he never completed his degree. In 1951, the absentee monarch and his queen finally announced they were returning to Thailand by sea. In a carefully timed counterstrike against the royalists on 29 November, just days before the king was due to arrive, Phibun suspended parliament and abrogated the 1949 constitution. On 2 December, when Bhumibol stepped ashore in Bangkok, he was a humiliated, politically emasculated monarch with a purely symbolic role.

The United States was now firmly established as the dominant international power in Thailand. It had little interest in promoting democracy. Washington wanted strong leaders who could assist the fight against communism. Phibun's junta seemed ideal, and billions of dollars of US aid and military assistance began flowing into Thailand. Phibun's sidekick Phao Sriyanond transformed the police into a paramilitary force that rivalled the army led by Sarit Thanarat. The ruling triumvirate entrenched their control over Thai politics and the national economy, and Sarit and Phao used their forces – paid for with US money – to battle for control of the opium trade.

The monarchy seemed destined to fade into irrelevance. But everything changed for Bhumibol when Sarit seized power in September 1957, banishing Phibun and Phao into exile abroad. The royalists had approved Sarit's plans in advance, and Bhumibol swiftly gave the coup his blessing. Sarit redefined the relationship between the monarchy and the military. As Thak Chaloemtiarana says in his seminal study of the period, it was the beginning of a partnership between Bhumibol and the army that was to dominate Thailand's post-war history. Sarit was an alcoholic and a shameless womanizer – 'practically no-one was immune to his overtures – beauty queens, movie stars, night club hostesses, university and secondary school students, the young and not so young' (Thak, 2007) – but he was an ideal ally for the young Bhumibol, treating the monarch respectfully and reviving dying traditions of reverence for the palace. The practice of prostration before the monarch was reintroduced. Bhumibol was still power-less, but the elite now showed him exaggerated respect instead of scorning him.

By 1958, Sarit had scrapped the constitution, abolished parliament, suspended elections, and tightened limitations on free speech. But just as kings had done from Chulalongkorn onwards, he insisted that in spite of all the evidence to the contrary, his despotic rule was a Thai style of democracy best suited to the country's cultural traditions and socio-economic realities. He proclaimed:

> I am a confirmed upholder of the principle of the ancient Thai administrative system of paternalistic rule. I love to refer to the fact that a nation is like one big family. The ruler is none other than the head of that big family who must regard all the people as his own children and grandchildren. He must be kind, compassionate and very mindful of their well-being.

In reality, as Kobkua observes, Sarit's democracy 'for all its virtuous intents and purposes was in practice the rule of military dictatorship' (Kobkua, 2003). But it was a military dictatorship that glorified Bhumibol.

The United States was delighted with this arrangement. In a secret cable, ambassador Alexis Johnson referred without apparent irony to the State Department's view that 'authoritarianism will remain the norm in Free Asia for a long period':

> We need not ... feel self-conscious about our support of an authoritarian government in Thailand based almost entirely on military strength... Aside from the practical matter of Thailand's not being ready for a truly democratic form of government, it can be pointed out that the United States derives political support from the Thai Government to an extent and degree which it would be hard to match elsewhere. Furthermore, the generally conservative nature of Thai military and governmental leaders and of long-established institutions (monarchy, Buddhism) furnish a strong barrier against the spread of Communist influence. (611.90/10–2059)

Sarit encouraged the royal couple to travel around the country; the rapturous welcome they received in rural areas demonstrated the persistence of old beliefs that the monarch was a semi-divine figure. The Western media joined in the deification of Thailand's fairy-tale king and queen. But real power lay with the army and the United States. Sarit – and Washington – saw Bhumibol as a puppet whose popularity and sacred aura of royalty could be usefully harnessed to legitimize their control.

The political and economic dominance of the United States transformed Thailand in the decades after World War II. The influx of US investment fuelled a long economic boom. The domestic engines of economic growth were banks mostly owned by ethnic Chinese families which scooped up the savings of rural

Thais and lent them to corporate entrepreneurs – also mostly ethnic Chinese. The palace played a central role in bringing Thai Chinese tycoons into the charmed circle of the royalist elite (Gray, 1986) and was also directly involved in business through the Crown Property Bureau. The Crown Property Act of 1948 had declared that control of CPB assets and income 'depends totally on the royal inclination' and absolved it of paying any tax. As Porphant Ouyyanont observes, the CPB is 'an absolutely unique entity ... difficult to define in terms of Thai law'. Its wealth was built on three main pillars – ownership of huge tracts of land, Siam Commercial Bank and Siam Cement (Porphant, 2008). Sarit's military also forged links with the old establishment through its stakes in state businesses. Little of the economic growth trickled down to the poor, and income inequality exploded (Glassman, 2004).

Sarit died in 1963, aged 55, ravaged by decades of alcoholism. A few months later, a family inheritance dispute brought the epic scale of his corruption into the open. An investigation uncovered assets of more than $140 million he had stolen to invest in business and maintain dozens of mistresses, many of whom were given a house, car and salary. The *New York Times* reported that his family controlled at least fifteen companies, including 'a bank with the monopoly of importing gold into Thailand, a construction concern that received major government contracts, a brewery, and a concession for the sale of the state lottery tickets'. He also owned fifty-one cars, a helicopter and a fishing boat (*New York Times*, 1969).

Sarit's successors at the helm of the junta, field marshals Thanom Kittikachorn and Praphas Charusathien, shared his flair for corruption. Meanwhile, as Anderson notes, 'the huge

American presence was generating serious social problems –
rampant prostitution, fatherless mixed-blood babies, drug ad-
diction, pollution, and sleazy commercialization of many aspects
of Thai life' (Anderson, 1977). All these issues fuelled growing
discontent among Thailand's poor. Rural resistance mounted
during the 1960s, and the underground Communist Party of
Thailand (CPT) capitalized on the discontent, as David Morell
and Chai-anan Samudavanija explain:

> Usually considered second-class citizens by the residents of
> Bangkok and the Central Plain, the Northeasterners ... developed
> a negative attitude towards central government officials. These
> tensions grew as more officials of the Bangkok regime were sent to
> the Northeast and their contacts with local villagers increased.

After years of neglect followed by problems with officials of the
central regime, numerous politically conscious north-easterners
were receptive to the appeals of the communist insurgents, who
offered their protection against local officials' abuse of power
and a chance for greater social mobility than was possible under
the traditional system. By the early 1960s, the CPT was able to
convince many villagers in this region that the Bangkok regime
no longer warranted their loyalty (Morell and Chai-anan, 1981).

The CPT launched an armed insurgency in 1965. By 1973,
several villages in the north-east were entirely under communist
control. But, besides genuine insurgent and political activities by
the CPT, any attempt by rural people to challenge their unequal
position in Thai society tended to be branded 'communist' and
'un-Thai', and brutally put down by the state. The demonization
of all insurgents as communists was also used to mask the fact
that ethnic Malay Muslims in southern Thailand were rebel-
ling against Bangkok rule too. To combat rural resistance, the

Thai military was given even more power and influence in the mid-1960s through the creation of the Internal Security Operations Command (ISOC), a sprawling and secretive institution with wide-ranging powers to crush dissent through force and propaganda.

To try to combat communism and win rural hearts and minds, the king launched his 'Royal Projects' in the 1960s, making trips to remote areas to talk to villagers and theatrically fix their problems. As even hagiographic accounts of Bhumibol's development activities have unwittingly shown (Grossman and Faulder, 2011) his approach was strikingly amateurish. Destinations were decided at the last minute, little research was done, and there was no overarching strategy. As Thongchai says,

> The truth about these projects, and their successes and failures, will probably remain unknown for years to come, given that public accountability and transparency for royal activities is unthinkable. Suffice it to say that the endlessly repeated images of the monarch travelling through remote areas, walking tirelessly along dirt roads, muddy paths and puddles, with maps, pens and a notebook in hand, a camera and sometimes a pair of binoculars around his neck, are common in the media, in public buildings and private homes. These images have captured the popular imagination during the past several decades. Bhumibol is portrayed as a popular king, a down-to-earth monarch who works tirelessly for his people. (Thongchai, 2008)

The king had limited understanding of rural problems; while his solutions were hailed as genius by the media, in fact he made little difference (Chanida, 2007). Royal propaganda was exceptionally successful, however: images of the king's rural travels were shown on daily royal news broadcasts on all television channels, and many Thais continue to believe that nobody has done more for ordinary people than their king.

Bhumibol was comfortable with military rule, but enjoyed his latitude to criticize the junta. It helped bolster his popular appeal, without requiring real change. He regarded the messy world of democracy with distaste. 'I became king when I was quite young. I was 18, and very suddenly, I learned that politics is a filthy business', he told *Life* magazine, repeating the fiction that the monarchy was inherently democratic: 'I really am an elected king. If the people do not want me, they can throw me out, eh? Then I will be out of a job' (Zimmerman, 1967). But he was taken by surprise when popular discontent with the junta exploded in 1973, and he found himself forced to endorse an end to military dictatorship. Suddenly, democracy in Thailand seemed possible once again.

The brief democratic interlude that followed the 1973 uprising was unruly and unstable. Students and unions held frequent protests and strikes. Elections were held in 1975 and 1976, contested by dozens of parties, which meant the parliaments they selected were fractious and weak. Nevertheless, Thailand had a democratically elected National Assembly for the first time since the 1940s. Meanwhile, multiple military atrocities were uncovered and publicized. In 1974, the village of Ban Na Sai in Nong Khai province was razed to the ground. The military authorities blamed communists, but student investigations showed ISOC was responsible (Mallett, 1978). In 1975, student activists uncovered the 'red drum' killings in the southern province of Patthalung in 1971–72. Thousands of local villagers had been arrested, interrogated and killed, incinerated in gasoline-filled oil drums – often while still alive (Peagam, 1975).

The palace and conservative royalists were in a state of 'genuine cultural-ideological panic' (Anderson, 1977). Students

The student uprising of 1973

In October 1973, the arrest of thirteen student activists provoked unprecedented mass protests on the streets of Bangkok. Up to half a million people rallied on 13 October, by far the biggest mass demonstration in Thai history. Students led the protest, but thousands of workers also joined them to denounce the government. The king extracted from the junta a promise to produce a new constitution within a year – hardly a major concession – and told the protesters to get off the streets. The following day, with huge crowds thronging Bangkok's royal quarter, the junta ordered military units to fire on protesters. At least seventy people were killed. Desperately trying to escape the bloodshed, some students clambered over the walls of Chitralada Palace. They were given sanctuary by the royal family. Thongchai describes what happened:

> Probably the most important act that symbolically defined the monarchy in Thai politics was on the morning of 14 October when demonstrators who were beaten by police in the street beside the palace climbed over the fence seeking refuge inside the palace ground. Then, the royal family in informal dress came out to meet and expressed sympathy to students. By the evening, the military junta had been forced out, thanks to a rival faction within the military that gained the upper hand, and – it is said – to an agreement between the junta and the palace. A grim-faced King Bhumipol appeared on television and declared 14 October 'the Most Tragic Day', and appointed as prime minister the President of his Privy Council. (Thongchai, 2008)

The junta leaders fled Thailand. It was a watershed moment in the country's history – a popular uprising had succeeded in forcing political change. Bhumibol had never wanted such a radical outcome and had been wrong-footed by events, eventually deciding to help engineer the departure of the junta to prevent further bloodshed. Yet he won immense adulation for his perceived support of democracy. Handley describes how the events of October 1973 became a seminal moment in terms of fostering Bhumibol's image as a 'democratic' monarch who ruled for the good of the people:

> October 14 has ever since taken on legendary proportions, in Thai consciousness and in Bhumibol's own record. To the students of that and succeeding generations, it was an unprecedented people's uprising against tyranny...

In official histories, however, it was the king who had single-handedly restored constitutionalism and democracy. Rather than credit the popular uprising, later books and articles overwhelmingly emphasized King Bhumibol's intervention against the dictators, saving the country from disaster.

'However it was characterized', Handley observes, 'the October 1973 uprising marked a new zenith in the restoration of the throne's power and grandeur.' (Handley, 2006a)

were lecturing their elders. Workers and peasants were demanding their rights. As a confidential cable from US ambassador Charles Whitehouse observed,

> Since the October 1973 change in government, Thailand has experienced considerable agitation for, if little real progress toward, a more just society with a wider distribution of economic benefits. Such turbulence has led to a certain amount of disorder, which the conservatives view as bordering on anarchy. Leftist agitation has stimulated a reaction, and the Thai political life has experienced distinct polarization over the past few months. (1975BANGKO18375)

Bhumibol's inclination towards authoritarianism left him perplexed and panicked by the forces that had been unleashed. The king had thought he could control the students and was shocked to find how wrong he was. Vientiane, Phnom Penh and Saigon all fell to communist forces in 1975. Meanwhile, popular pressure forced the withdrawal of US forces in 1976, adding to the paranoia of the palace. Bhumibol and Sirikit aligned themselves firmly with the extreme right. They developed close links with a secretive group called Nawapol, a cabal of senior members of the military, bureaucracy, judiciary, Buddhist hierarchy and business elite organized by ISOC. The palace also played a central role in fostering a far-right rural mass movement, the Village Scouts, taking an active part in their indoctrination rituals (Bowie, 1997).

In September 1976, the king allowed exiled dictator Thanom to return to Thailand. It was a calculated challenge by the reactionary right against supporters of democracy. Thanom was ordained as a monk in Wat Bovornives, the Bangkok temple most closely linked to the royal family. Following furious protests by students and the elected government, Bhumibol and Sirikit personally visited him there to show their support for his return. It was a provocative gesture that inflamed tensions still further and widened Thailand's political divisions. Thousands of protesting students gathered inside the campus of Thammasat University. On 5 October, spurred on by radio broadcasts accusing the students of *lèse-majesté* and communism, thousands of royalist paramilitaries massed outside the campus. Shortly before sunrise on 6 October, the massacre began:

> At 5.30 a.m. a rocket-propelled bomb was fired into the crowd inside Thammasat. It was reported that four were killed instantly and dozens injured. That bomb signalled the beginning of the nonstop discharge of military weapons which lasted until about 9 a.m. Anti-tank missiles were fired into the Commerce building which by then sheltered a third of the crowd. Outside the university, after the besieging forces had stormed into the campus, they dragged some students out. Lynching began. Two were tortured, hanged

and beaten even after death on the trees encircling Sanam Luang...
the huge public space that separates Thammasat from the Grand
Palace by only a two minute walking distance. A female student,
chased until she fell to the ground, was sexually assaulted and
tortured until she died. On the street in front of the Ministry of
Justice, on the other side of Sanam Luang opposite Thammasat,
three bodies, alive but unconscious, were piled up with tyres,
soaked with petrol, then set alight. These brutal murders took
place as a public spectacle. Many of the onlookers, including young
boys, clapped their hands in joy. (Thongchai, 2002)

Another brief, doomed experiment with democracy was over,
crushed by the right wing of the ruling class with the full support
of the monarchy.

SIX

'There is magic, goodness and power in his heart'
The deification of Rama IX

Around 9:30 p.m. on 20 May 1992, an extraordinary scene was shown on Thai television. Within a few hours it was dominating news broadcasts around the world. Dressed in a tan suit and sitting on a couch, King Rama IX was quietly lecturing two men who prostrated themselves at his feet and then knelt submissively on the floor as Bhumibol admonished them. One of them was Suchinda Kraprayoon, the de facto leader of a military junta that seized power in a coup in 1991 and then engineered his election as prime minister. The other was Chamlong Srimuang, an eccentric former general and governor of Bangkok who was a devotee of an ascetic Buddhist sect and had led mass protests against Suchinda's government. Over the preceding three days, the military had sought to crush dissent, with troops opening fire on unarmed protesters on the streets of Bangkok, killing dozens and wounding hundreds. Thailand seemed on the brink of even deadlier unrest, until Bhumibol summoned Suchinda and Chamlong to his palace and ordered them to settle their differences. There was no further violence.

It was the most legendary episode of Bhumibol's reign. 'By the early 1990s signs of Rama IX's incipient apotheosis were aplenty, but none more eloquent than the televised royal audience on 20 May 1992', observes Peleggi. 'Fifty million TV spectators watched Suchinda and Chamlong kneeling at the king's feet ... and humbly receiving the royal admonition to take a step back and stop the violence in the streets' (Peleggi, 2009). The *Washington Post* was effusive in its praise:

> Who will soon forget the remarkable picture of the military ruler and the opposition leader together on their knees before the king of Thailand? Summoning up the impartiality and sense of national essence that he has cultivated for 42 years on an otherwise powerless throne, King Bhumibol Adulyadej was able at least to ease the immediate confrontation between Suchinda Kraprayoon, the general who is prime minister, and Chamlong Srimuang, the former general who leads the opposition. At once Thailand's boiling crisis was moved from the streets to the political bargaining table. (*Washington Post*, 1992)

But the irony was that – just as in 1973 – Bhumibol had not been on the side of the people at all. Throughout the crisis he had supported Suchinda and the army, exhibiting the ingrained preference for military rather than civilian rule that has always characterized his reign. In his televised dressing down of the prime minister and the protest leader, Bhumibol referred derisively to 'so-called democracy', and directed most of his criticism at Chamlong rather than at Suchinda. For the second time in his reign, Thailand's anti-democratic king found himself credited for taking decisive action to restore democracy.

Like most of the traditional ruling class, Bhumibol had always been contemptuous of the notion of letting ordinary people determine how the country should be run. His political philosophy was antithetical to equality and democracy, based instead upon a belief in enlightened leadership by a morally superior elite. But the king and the old establishment continued to insist that their rule was somehow more democratic than systems involving elections and popular sovereignty. They described their dominance as 'democracy with the king as head of state', also known as 'Thai-style democracy', and claimed it was the political system best suited to Thailand. In fact, of course, Thai-style democracy was not democracy at all.

Following the slaughter at Thammasat University in 1976, the elected government was replaced by an appointed administration led by Tanin Kraivixien, a close confidante of Bhumibol and Sirikit. Thousands of students fled the cities to join communist insurgents in the jungle. The monarchy faced a crisis, and secret US and British cables from the weeks after the massacre report that Bhumibol and his circle were anxiously questioning diplomats about how the palace could repair its shattered image. The penalties for *lèse-majesté* were increased, and royal propaganda intensified. The absurdly exaggerated worship of the palace, which Thongchai calls 'hyper-royalism', began during this period. As he says, 'the huge industry of royal deification was elevated to an unprecedented level following the 1976 massacre, which was seen among the right-wing royalists as a decisive victory over the communism that threatened to end the monarchy' (Thongchai, 2008). Thais – particularly the elite – competed to be as ostentatiously royalist as possible, leading to a phenomenon that political scientist Xavier Marquez has dubbed 'flattery inflation' (Marquez, 2013).

The royal family's support for Tanin's government was another disaster – he proved so extremist and incompetent that he was overthrown by a moderate military faction in 1977. Recognition of the damaging consequences of the palace's lurch to the extreme right persuaded Bhumibol and his circle that a more moderate form of elite rule was required. In 1980, the palace engineered the ascent of a new prime minister: royalist general Prem Tinsulanonda. He served as premier for eight years, overseeing the construction of another incarnation of 'Thai-style' faux democracy. Regular elections were held from 1979 onwards, but Prem never deigned to go before voters himself. Parliament's influence was sharply constrained, and the military was given an exalted position. Power still lay with an oligarchy of generals, tycoons, senior bureaucrats and judges. At the heart of the elite was Prem, acting as the chief consigliere of the palace:

> High-society Thais and ambitious climbers competed ever more
> to be seen donating funds and participating in royal events. They
> sought to take part in a full-fledged court society fostered by Prem,
> centered in part in the Dusit Thani Hotel. The Dusit became
> the site of regular royal charity balls, its restaurants preferred by
> Sirikit, Prem, and their circle of royally decorated ladies. It became
> the place for businessmen, politicians, generals, and their wives to
> be seen and do business. (Handley, 2006a)

Royal wealth was used to bind together the establishment. The Crown Property Bureau diversified into a dizzying array of businesses. 'By the closing stages of the great boom, the CPB had become a sprawling conglomerate. According to estimates, the CPB had direct interests in around 90 companies, and indirect interests in another 300', writes Porphant. 'The CPB owned one of the largest (perhaps *the* largest) corporate groups in Thailand' (Porphant, 2008).

Parliament was a sideshow, another example of the use of theatrics to mask the real distribution of power. As David Murray explains:

> To add a veneer of political legitimacy to the power structure,
> from time to time political parties and a parliamentary system of
> government have been allowed to operate, usually under prescribed
> conditions whereby politicians and parliament have been relegated
> to the position of a bit player on the margins of central decision
> making. As soon as the politicians have overstepped the bounds

placed on their role, the armed forces have mounted yet another successful coup and the country has lapsed yet again into a period of undemocratic government. (Murray, 1996)

Parliamentary politics became dominated by sleazy political 'godfathers', mostly provincial strongmen who had developed local patronage networks to support their underground activities. They were perfectly placed to profit from the emergence of electoral competition – through connections and coercion they could control a large number of votes. 'Once elected, they treated politics as a kind of business, effectively selling public policy, office, concession or title deed to the highest bidder', observes Kasian (2006). It was the poor – perennial victims of Thailand's corrupt politics – who were officially blamed for this sad state of affairs. They were accused of being too uneducated to make sensible electoral choices, and of selling their votes to the highest bidder (Callahan, 2005; Bowie, 2008). This was nonsense. It was the elite who perpetuated – and profited from – corruption.

Prem's eight years in office were characterized by vicious infighting among factions of the elite for a bigger share of the wealth created by a long export-driven boom that lasted well into the 1990s. He survived two coup attempts thanks to the direct intervention of the palace to protect him, demonstrating that Bhumibol was by no means obliged to acquiesce to every attempted putsch.

By the late 1980s, the elite no longer felt threatened by communism, and pressure was growing from more liberal members of the establishment and the expanding middle class for more representative government. Prem stepped down as prime minister in 1988, weakened by several corruption scandals and a humiliating defeat for the military in a border war with Laos. Bhumibol immediately appointed him the effective head of the privy council, the king's advisory body of elderly men, which wields significant power among the elite. The basic power structure in Thailand remained unchanged. McCargo has famously characterized it as 'network monarchy':

> The main features of Thailand's network monarchy ... were as follows: the monarch was the ultimate arbiter of political decisions in times of crisis; the monarchy was the primary source of national legitimacy; the King acted as a didactic commentator on national issues, helping to set the national agenda, especially through his annual birthday speeches; the monarch intervened actively in political developments, largely by working through proxies such as privy councillors and trusted military figures; and the lead proxy, former army commander and prime minister Prem Tinsulanond, helped determine the nature of coalition governments, and monitored the process of military and other promotions. At heart, network governance of this kind relied on placing the right people (mainly, the right men) in the right jobs...
>
> Network monarchy is inherently illiberal, because it advocates reliance on 'good men', and the marginalization of formal political institutions or procedures. Low priority is given to democratic principles such as the rule of law and popular sovereignty. (McCargo, 2005)

The prime minister who followed was Chatichai Choonhavan, scion of an elite family. His government was equally corrupt but gave more power to civilian politicians to loot the country rather than army officers. It became known as the 'buffet cabinet' for the enthusiasm with which ministers helped themselves to the spoils of office. The military soon decided it was time for another coup. Suchinda's junta seized power in 1991 with the approval of the king. The coup leaders promised to clean up Thai politics and restore democracy. When these claims proved hollow, the network monarchy was blindsided by another mass uprising – this time by the middle class.

The middle-class revolt of Black May 1992

After seizing power from the elected government in 1991, Suchinda's junta began work on a new constitution. The proposed charter was a severe setback for democracy, with several clauses designed to perpetuate military dominance of politics even after elections were held. 'Ever since the military overthrew the oppressive civilian regime of Tanin Kraivixien more than a decade ago, we have cherished the hope that never again would our country slide back into such a dark age', said the *Bangkok Post* in a front-page editorial. 'Never again, we told ourselves, would the Thai people be treated with such disdain and their democratic aspirations taken for granted by the military elite.' The newspaper noted the junta had promised 'a new political era under which the next election would be free and fair, politicians would be less corrupt and, above all, a fully democratic parliament would emerge', adding: 'This now appears to be a cruel delusion' (*Bangkok Post*, 1991). On 19 November, more than 70,000 people rallied in protest against the proposed charter, the biggest mass demonstration since 1973. A survey in December by the Campaign for Popular Democracy found 98.8 per cent of 312,357 people polled were against the draft constitution. Popular momentum was building to demand more democracy. Then the king abruptly shattered these aspirations. In his 1991 birthday speech he argued that no political system was flawless, and that for a poor country like Thailand compromise and unity were more important than trying to create an idealistic constitution based on ideals about democracy imported from abroad. He told Thais to cease their protests. If there were problems with the constitution, Bhumibol said, they could always be fixed later.

Elections were set for March 1992 and pro-military parties won a majority of seats. Suchinda, who had previously promised to step aside after democracy was restored, announced he would have to become prime minister after all to 'save the nation', weeping as he spoke. He proceeded to name a cabinet filled with cronies, shady political godfathers, and several legislators whom the junta had denounced and investigated for unusual wealth only a year before. As McCargo observes:

> Here was parliamentary dictatorship in its ultimate form: a parliament whose election had been orchestrated by a dictatorship, which then presented the premiership to a dictator. The greatest shock of all came when Suchinda announced his cabinet. The very same politicians he had decried a year earlier as 'unusually rich' were now sitting around his cabinet table, in a scene strongly reminiscent of the final pages of Orwell's Animal Farm. (McCargo, 2001)

Bangkok's middle class and business community were outraged. Most newspapers denounced Suchinda – *The Nation* said he had achieved 'a standard of hypocrisy that is hard to surpass' (*The Nation*, 1992). The Thai stock market went into freefall, and, as political turmoil worsened, a pro-democracy protest movement emerged. Chamlong Srimuang led several rallies of tens of thousands of Thais in late April and early May. The protesters were denounced by Suchinda and his allies as communists and anti-monarchists. They were anything but. Most were staunch royalists and many were from the newly affluent middle classes. David Murray reports that their nicknames included 'the mobile phone mob', the 'picnic mob', the 'yoghurt-drink mob' and the 'yuppie mob'. 'Many demonstrators brought with them their own provisions', he explains. 'Instead of bullet proof vests and gas masks, they came armed with bags of drinks and snacks, portable stereo sets and mattresses' (Murray, 1996). Bhumibol appeared wrong-footed by the protests, continuing to back the military even as more and more Thais joined mass rallies. On the evening of 17 May, some 200,000 people filled Sanam Luang. Chamlong led them on a march towards Government House, but they were blocked by razor-wire barricades at the Phan Fa bridge. Scuffles broke out, and dozens of protesters and police were wounded. In the early hours of 18 May, the government declared a state of emergency. As the violence worsened, soldiers fired M16 assault rifles directly into the crowd. Several people were killed. Protesters refused to disperse and defiantly raised their hands in the air to show they were unarmed. During the afternoon, Suchinda appeared on television to declare the government had no choice but to use whatever force necessary. Murray recounts the events of that day:

> About 10,000 protesters remained milling around outside the Public Relations Department. By 6:00 p.m. there were also 20,000 outside the Royal Hotel. They booed and jeered the troops, waving bloodied clothing and challenging the soldiers to open fire. The troops fired repeated volleys over their heads. By 8:30 p.m., the crowd had swollen dramatically, buses were commandeered, ... vehicles were set on fire, and large cement flower tubs lined up as barricades. The crowds continued to jeer, shouting anti-Suchinda slogans. Troops and demonstrators clashed in battles to control the area in front of the Public Relations Department. At 8:40 p.m., troops opened fire on about 30,000 protesters, and again at 10:20 p.m. On both occasions the firing was for sustained periods, and more than 30 were feared killed. Demonstrators covered the bodies of the dead with the national flag. In a video tape recording, an officer was heard to instruct the troops to shoot at will. The same footage showed a demonstrator who was running away cut down in a hail of automatic gunfire. The number of unarmed civilians killed in the rally remains unknown.

Around 5 a.m. on 19 May, troops stormed the Royal Hotel, which was being used as a makeshift medical centre to treat wounded protesters. They arrested thousands of protesters, taking them away in trucks. By 8:30 a.m., Murray reports, the resistance in Ratchadamnoen Avenue had been crushed:

> The Avenue was deserted. Smoke still curled from the shells of the government buildings that had been burned. Thousands of sandals were scattered about. The scorched, wrecked bodies of cars, pickup trucks, three petrol tankers and seven buses littered the street. The pavements and roadway were strewn with glass. (Murray, 1996)

Across Thailand and around the world, Bhumibol's failure to intervene seemed increasingly troubling and incomprehensible. It was widely assumed that the military must be holding him incommunicado. As *Time* reported:

> Bangkok ... was no longer a capital of prosperity. It was a city in shock – numbed by tumult, appalled at wholesale death in the streets and raging at a Prime Minister who had become the most hated man in Thailand. Throughout those three days, people looked imploringly to Chitralada Palace and the one figure capable of intervening decisively. Their long wait had begun to convince many Thais that King Bhumibol ... could not risk squandering his moral authority when words might not matter. Soldiers were at war with civilians. Both sides were digging in. A nation that had been basking in the sunlight of economic success looked headed for eclipse in further nights of the generals. (*Time*, 1992)

Finally, on 20 May, the palace acted. At 6 a.m., Sirindhorn appeared on television pleading for the killing to stop. That evening, Bhumibol made his famous intervention, and emerged from the episode with his reputation enhanced. Thailand's middle class revered the monarch more than ever. But their adulation was based on profound misunderstanding of his role in the crisis. As Chris Baker observes:

> Since the 1976 drama, an important section of the Thai elite and middle class has needed to imagine the king as a symbol of democracy, particularly in opposition to the soldiers who wanted to suppress it with guns, and the businessmen who wanted to subvert it with money. These people want to make use of the great moral authority of the monarchy, without paying attention to the politics. They have been complicit in rewriting history to cast the king as a peace-maker in 1973 and 1992, glossing over 1976 altogether, and ignoring the 1932 revolution to make democracy seem to be a gift from the throne. (Baker, 2006)

Once again, myths had triumphed over reality.

The events of May 1992 appeared to have ended overt military intervention in Thai politics. A series of unstable elected civilian governments followed, all generally corrupt and incompetent. Politicians remained junior members of the establishment, with real power still wielded by tycoons, bureaucrats and favourites of the palace. But the Black May uprising had demonstrated the inadequacies of royalist rule:

> Despite the general view that the violence of May 1992 signalled it was time to stop relying on the military and the monarchy, and highlighted the need for a process of thoroughgoing constitutional and political reform, all the evidence suggests that the King himself failed to understand this... The violence of May 1992 had left the King in an apparently strong position. He emerged as the supreme political referee, following a superficially successful intervention to solve the crisis. Yet the intervention also marked the high watermark of his authority. His consistent support for the military reflected an obsolete understanding of the Thai political and social order. (McCargo, 2005)

In his annual birthday speeches, the king castigated successive governments, channelling popular revulsion at the greed and ineptitude of politicians. He paid particular attention to two issues, both linked to old traditions of kingship. Bhumibol took a personal interest in management of water – central to the sacred role of monarchs in Ayutthaya – involving himself in flood prevention, dam projects and cloud-seeding rain-making initiatives. He also became very publicly involved in efforts to alleviate Bangkok's worsening traffic problems. Years of economic growth and incompetent urban planning had made the capital notorious for its paralysing gridlock. The monarchy worsened the problem because – again as in Ayutthaya centuries before – strict constraints were imposed on the population when royal convoys passed through the capital. Major roads were closed hours in advance, and so were flyovers and pedestrian over-passes to conform with the ancient stricture that subjects of the monarchy should not be physically higher than the king. The delays and inconvenience infuriated ordinary people – even am-bulances carrying the critically ill to hospital had to wait for hours like everybody else. The king began making theatrical efforts to improve traffic conditions, appearing regularly on television lecturing officials on transport management. 'It sounded good, but it didn't mean much', observes Handley. 'Some of the king's advice was useful, but mostly it echoed what was already being done. Some ideas were fundamentally wrong' (Handley, 2006a).

Meanwhile, the more liberal members of Thailand's estab-lishment recognized the need to lay foundations for longer-term stability and create a political system that would preserve elite dominance even after Bhumibol's death. They pressed for a new constitution that relied less on the monarchy and more on the elite network of 'good men' who effectively ran the country. Conservative royalists, however, were adamantly opposed to any constitutional changes that gave more power to parliament and diluted the power of the palace. As McCargo observes, 'The political reform agenda reflected a struggle between liberals and conservatives for the soul of network monarchy' (McCargo, 2005).

During 1997, it appeared that the conservatives would prevail. But a sudden and savage economic shock changed everything. The heady growth that had transformed Thailand since the mid-1980s had created a bubble mentality, compounded by the traditional cronyism of Thai business. Banks handed out loans with little oversight, and often the money was not invested for any productive purpose. Moreover, much of the foreign cash that had flooded into Thailand was 'hot money', invested in speculative short-term assets rather than productive capital. As Thailand's economic problems became more apparent, foreigners began yanking their money out. In May 1997, the rush to the exit became a stampede. The government dithered haplessly, eventually bowing to the inevitable and devaluing the baht on 2 July. Thailand's economy went into free fall, setting off a regional contagion that sparked panicked outflows from markets across Southeast Asia. International investors had lost faith in the supposedly miraculous economic prospects of the region, suddenly perceiving a darker reality of entrenched corruption and toxic crony capitalism. The fairy tale of Thailand's economic miracle had been abruptly punctured.

The crisis was catastrophic for the Crown Property Bureau. The overextended and highly leveraged Siam Cement and Siam Commercial Bank became technically bankrupt. They stopped paying dividends, as did most other firms in the CPB's portfolio. Its annual income collapsed by 75 per cent (Porphant, 2008). Reeling from the financial disaster, conservatives abandoned their opposition to a new charter. The so-called 'People's Constitution' was promulgated in October 1997. Although far from progressive, it was an improvement on previous arrangements. The power of the elected executive was strengthened to end years of weak revolving-door governments, and as a countermeasure several new institutions were created to act as checks and balances, staffed by elite grandees. 'In other words', observes McCargo, 'network monarchy could be reorganized on a firmer basis, transcending the informal subsystem that had existed until now' (McCargo, 2005). Michael Connors characterizes the system as 'royal liberalism': 'Thai liberal democracy has come to mean governments which rule by the consent of the people *when they are able to make the right choices*, where power is divided among the executive, legislature and judiciary, and the king plays a guardianship role, and holds ultimate sovereignty' (Connors, 2008). It was another incarnation of Thai-style democracy – despite the charade of elections and parliamentary government, power lay with the royalist oligarchy:

> The unwritten principles of the new constitution were simple: Good people would be able to enter politics, these good politicians would follow agreed rules of the game, they would not challenge the power or prestige of the monarchy, and in return the monarchy would not interfere with their activities. (McCargo, 2009)

Thailand's twentieth-century history appeared to be a very gradual and messy evolution towards greater democracy. There was still far to go, as Kobkua observes:

> Democracy practised in Thailand from 1932 to the 1990s is at best the rule of a benevolent despot, and at worst a system of power-sharing among greedy, self-centred and unscrupulous politicians and bureaucrats. Evidently the system had little to do with ordinary people who were allocated only an insignificant part in the overall political scheme of this power-struggling and power-sharing exercise among the ruling élite...
> In short, one may even go so far as to say that democracy has never really been attempted in Thailand. What has been established and seriously cultivated is a reverse form of democracy, a rule of oligarchy ... a system of absolute power among friends. That system has proved to be a total failure for the aspirations of modern Thailand. (Kobkua, 2003)

But the foundations seemed to have been laid for a more inclusive and democratic nation – albeit one in which the elite retained an exalted political role. The country was gradually recovering from the economic collapse, and the finances of the Crown Property Bureau had been repaired – leading elite bankers had been drafted in to help, and the government allowed Siam Commercial

Bank to recapitalize under highly favourable terms accorded to no other financial institution (Porphant, 2008). The military seemed to have retreated to the barracks and ended its incessant political meddling. Thailand was seen as a success story – and the local and international media were unanimous in giving the king the greatest credit.

In December 1999, Bhumibol celebrated his 72nd birthday – a particularly significant one, since Thai Buddhists measure their lives in 12-year cycles. A month of festivities marked the occasion. On the day itself – 5 December – Bangkok's new Skytrain elevated railway was officially opened. It was a partial solution to the interminable traffic jams that plagued the capital, but raised a thorny question of protocol – what would happen when a royal convoy travelled underneath? 'We have talked about this matter with the … royal palace', an official told the *New York Times*. 'The palace allows the Skytrain to run normally with no stop on this regard' (Olson, 1999). The monarchy, it seemed, was embracing modernity. In an effusive story praising the king, *Time* declared:

> The king is universally revered by the entire population of Thailand… In the villages, many are still too overawed even to look at him. Instead they put out handkerchiefs for him to walk on and save the scraps of cloth with his footprint in shrines at home.
> Thais have nothing but good things to say about their monarch: 'Thailand wouldn't be worth living in if we didn't have him', says Pim Sairattanee, also aged 72, a flower seller on Bangkok's busy Sukhumvit Road. 'He has a white heart, there is magic, goodness and power in his heart', adds Prachob Virawong, 42, a street vendor from the poor northeast who sells fried grasshoppers in Bangkok. When boxer Somluck Khamsing won Thailand's first ever Olympic gold medal in Atlanta in 1996, it was a portrait of the King that he raised over his head in celebration. Says Bangkok political scientist Chai-anan Samudavanija: 'He is perhaps the only monarch who anywhere who has total love and no fear.'

Besides the hagiographic portrait of Bhumibol, the magazine acknowledged a 'darker side' to the country's story: 'Thailand promotes itself through its national airline as smooth as silk. But all too often the silk has been shredded, as selfish, power-hungry, cynical men have torn the national fabric to satisfy personal ambition.' In tactful language, it noted widespread fears that Bhumibol's death would herald a troubled era for Thailand:

> Many Thais are uneasy at the thought that they may be living in the twilight of Bhumibol's reign. Even as the nation prepares to celebrate his 72nd birthday, thoughts of the future are tinged with foreboding. The 47-year-old Crown Prince Vajiralongkorn has yet to achieve the same level of devotion among Thais that his father enjoys, and some say the King has set an impossibly high standard to follow.

Despite these concerns, the magazine concluded that Bhumibol could congratulate himself on a job well done: 'after more than half a century of taxing rule, the King should be above such worries' (McCarthy, 1999). But the celebrations were premature. Behind the facade of the Land of Smiles, a succession struggle was brewing that would destroy the royalist myths of progress and bring Thailand to the brink of civil war.

PART III

The secrets of succession

SEVEN

'Endless struggles for the throne'
The causes of chronic palace conflict

The social and political conflict tearing twenty-first-century Thailand apart is so bitter and intractable that the opposing sides cannot even agree what they are fighting over. But there is remarkable unanimity among all the leading protagonists on what the struggle is not about. It has absolutely nothing, they insist, to do with the uniquely sensitive subject of looming royal succession when Bhumibol dies.

After Bangkok was convulsed by violence in 2010, the Ministry of Foreign Affairs helpfully issued a document for diplomats and journalists, answering several 'Frequently Asked Questions about the Current Political Situation in Thailand'. Question 10 was: 'Is the uncertainty associated with the issue of succession a destabilizing factor for the Thai situation?' The answer, according to the Ministry, was a resounding No:

> The issue of royal succession is clear, both with regard to the Heir to the Throne and rules and procedures as to what will happen should the need arise. Relevant provisions in the current Constitution also lay out the specific roles of the Privy Council, National Assembly and Cabinet.
> Nevertheless, the succession is certainly a difficult issue for Thais to discuss, given what His Majesty has done for more than 60 years for the well-being of all Thai people who regard him as a father figure. It is thus normal for people to be apprehensive. (Ministry of Foreign Affairs, 2010)

Abhisit Vejjajiva, the patrician Eton- and Oxford-educated leader of the Democrat Party, who became prime minister in controversial circumstances in late 2008, made similar points when asked about the succession at the Foreign Correspondents' Club of Hong Kong:

> If you look at succession issues, there are two things that we should accept. The first is that if there are clear rules for succession. That eliminates a lot of uncertainty around how the succession process will actually evolve or work out. There are clear constitutional provisions, so in that sense, that eliminates some of the uncertainty.
> The second issue is undebatable. When you have had a leader for more than six decades and one that has built up so much reverence and respect from the people, there's always going to be anxiety. I don't know of any country or society or even organization where there has been an inspirational leader who has been there for a long time that does not have anxiety about succession. But Thailand has to make sure that we are mature enough as a country to deal with changes, economic, political and whatever issues that we need to face. I have no illusion that when it happens, it will be a very difficult time for all of us because we are very much attached to His Majesty. But we have to prove our maturity as a people and as a society and demonstrate to the rest of the world that we can deal with all issues and changes. (Ministry of Foreign Affairs, 2009)

Abhisit's political nemesis is Thaksin Shinawatra, whom he blames for everything that has gone wrong in Thailand (Abhisit, 2013). But one thing they don't appear to disagree on is royal succession. Discussing the issue in an interview with *The Times* at his Dubai villa, where he was living in exile, Thaksin declared:

> The King is the most respected person. He's become god in the feelings of the Thai people... Thailand's been governed by this dynasty more than 200 years. There's going to be a smooth transition but Thais need to reconcile their differences first, before the reign change. The reign change will be smooth. (Lloyd Parry, 2009)

Speaking to Bloomberg News in 2012, Thaksin stuck to the same story: 'There shouldn't be any problem about the succession of the throne. There is nothing to worry' (Ten Kate, 2012).

So the message from Thailand's elite on both sides of the conflict is clear. Bhumibol's death may be a traumatic shock for many Thais, but there is no disagreement over who will succeed him – Crown Prince Vajiralongkorn is the designated heir, and the succession will proceed smoothly according to clearly established rules. 'There is thus no cause for uncertainty and no warranted basis for speculation otherwise' says the Ministry of Foreign Affairs (Ministry of Foreign Affairs, 2011).

Journalists and academics have overwhelmingly taken these claims at face value. But they are completely untrue. Throughout centuries of Thai history, the royal succession has nearly always been violently contested and the rules have almost invariably been broken. Contemporary Thailand is no different. A bitter battle over royal succession is at the heart of the country's turmoil.

Thailand's destiny has always been defined by two parallel conflicts. For centuries, the ruling class has sought to oppress and exploit ordinary people, who have struggled for greater freedom and a fairer society. And for centuries there has been continual feuding and tension among different factions of the establishment fighting to preserve and expand their power. Scholars have long struggled to define 'the state' in premodern and contemporary Southeast Asia, but the best way to understand it is to view it as a loose coalition of powerful families who monopolize power over generations. The dominant clans compete relentlessly, and the oligarchy is continually changing as some families rise and others fall, but despite their constant feuding they share a common interest in maintaining elite rule. Quaritch Wales observes that during the era of absolute monarchy, members of the ruling class 'were continually occupied in showing the necessary amount of deference to those above them, and to the king at the top, while mercilessly grinding down those below them in the social scale' – a description that still holds true today (Quaritch Wales, 1931). But their veneration of the monarchy has always tended to be posturing, a pragmatic strategy to maintain their supremacy rather than a genuine expression of reverence for royalty. The elite prefer monarchs who can command sufficient respect from the populace to hold the kingdom together, but who are weak enough to be puppets of the ruling class rather than their masters. Behind their theatrical obsequiousness to the palace, they want kings they can control.

For elite families seeking to secure their dominance over the centuries, management of royal successions was crucial. They competed to play the role of 'kingmaker' – placing a monarch on the throne who would protect and reward them – and did their best to sabotage the rise of rulers who could threaten the power and prestige they had accumulated. The self-legitimizing Hindu and Buddhist theologies adopted by the ruling class in the region fuelled conflict over royal succession, because of an inherent paradox in the ideology that those who held power had earned it from accumulated *karma* – those who lost power were believed to have deserved that, too. Usurpers could further legitimize themselves by fostering an image of great wisdom and virtue, bolstered by ritualistic displays of piety that created the impression that they conformed to the ideals of kingship. Another legitimizing strategy was to win physical possession of the palace and of sacred artefacts and palladia. It was widely believed that force alone could not win control of palaces and artefacts imbued with sacred power – only the righteous could possess them. All of this was a recipe for regular eruptions of violence and intra-elite conflict since the earliest Southeast Asian kingdoms. As Robert Heine-Geldern observed in a classic article on kingship:

> the theory of divine incarnation, and even more so that of rebirth and of karma, provided an easy subterfuge for usurpers. The fact that the relatively easy task of seizing the palace, as in Burma and Siam, or of seizing the regalia, as in certain parts of Indonesia, often sufficed to be accepted as king by the whole nation, was bound to act as an additional incitement to rebellion. Moreover, the immense power and the lack of restrictions which the king enjoyed invited abuses which in the end made the monarch obnoxious to his subjects and hastened his downfall.
>
> To this came the vagueness of the rules of succession. Sometimes the king himself chose his successor. Sometimes the ministers appointed a prince as king. Then again the queens unofficially but efficiently exercised their influence in favor of a prince of their choice. Often the crown simply fell to the prince who was the quickest to seize the palace and to execute his brothers. Under these circumstances it is no wonder that the empires of Southeast Asia from the very beginning were torn by frequent rebellion, often resulting in the overthrow of kings or even dynasties. (Heine-Geldern, 1956)

After Ayutthaya's first king, Ramathibodi, died in 1369, his son reigned for less than a year before being forced to abdicate by an uncle. 'This was the first of many occasions ... when an uncle would seize his nephew's inheritance', wrote Prince Chula Chakrabongse in *Lords of Life*, a twentieth-century chronicle of Siam's monarchy which conceded that the history of Ayutthaya 'was one of endless struggles for the throne by the different claimants as no definite rule of succession was laid down' (Chula, 1960). The losers were routinely massacred.

The formulation and enforcement of rules specifying a clear line of succession could have ameliorated these frequent bouts of bloodletting, but an inherent tension in all systems of hereditary succession is that the more rigid the rules, the more random the quality of a country's kings. Improving the odds of having acceptable monarchs requires building some flexibility into the system and widening the pool of potential candidates, but this creates more conflict. For this reason, as Robert L. Solomon argues, monarchies in the region have always tended to be characterized by 'vagueness of succession': 'Southeast Asian practice – and ideal – regarding royal succession kept within the two poles of standardization of rules (which makes the transfer of office a smoother, more acceptable affair) and flexibility (necessary to maintain a minimal level of competence and adequacy)' (Solomon, 1970).

The interests of kings and the wider nobility were misaligned with respect to royal succession. Kings generally wanted succession rules to be strictly observed, thus minimizing the risk of a usurpation, maximizing their chances of dying a natural rather than a violent death, and, after that, enabling their chosen successor to smoothly take power. The nobility wanted enough flexibility to enable them to influence the succession and strive to ensure that candidates favourable to their interests prevailed. Succession conflicts also suited the nobility because they prevented the royal family from becoming too powerful relative to the rest of the elite. Weakened by regular intrafamilial slaughter and the need to maintain support among the nobility, reigning dynasties found it more difficult to consolidate power in the palace.

Several historians have noted the tendency of the power of Southeast Asian monarchies to wax and wane as a result of systemic tensions with the wider elite. A powerful king could seek to centralize power, exert more control over the nobility and demand more tax revenue for the palace and more labour from the population. But as dynasties weakened due to infighting over the succession and elite machinations to put pliant monarchs on the throne, power seeped away from the palace. Officials in the capital and the leaders of regional vassal cities would carve out more autonomy for themselves and keep a greater share of tax revenue and bonded labour. From time to time, a king would emerge who found a way to centralize power once again – often by seizing the throne by force and massacring the most powerful members of the old nobility – and the cycle would begin again. This was the reason for the concertina-like expansion and contraction of *mandala* states noted by Wolters.

King Trailok, who reigned for four decades from 1448, was an early centralizing monarch, as Wood explains in his *History of Siam*:

> Until the time of King Trailok, the different provinces of the Kingdom, whether presided over by Princes or by officials of lower rank, had been governed more or less like small independent States, levying their armies, controlling their own finances, and managing their own internal affairs. King Trailok made the first attempt at centralisation. At the same time he brought about a separation between the civil and military administration, which had been closely interwoven. He raised the rank of the principle officials ... and placed them in charge of different Departments for the control of the affairs of the whole Kingdom. (Wood, 1926)

An important element of Trailok's palace law of 1456 was a rule on royal succession, specifying that upon the death of a king, sons whose mother had the status of full queen rather than concubine would be first in line for the throne. These princes had the special title of *chao fa*, usually translated as 'celestial prince'. If there were none, the throne could pass to other relatives of the monarch. Trailok also established the position of *uparaja*, or deputy king, who would be appointed by the monarch to assist him in governing and – in theory – help with ensuring a smooth succession.

In practice, these refinements failed to end Ayutthaya's cycle of regular savage succession struggles. There were too many incentives for the nobility to seek to circumvent the rules. But the problem was not – as many historians wrongly surmise – that the law on succession was ambiguous. It was perfectly clear, but usually ignored:

> The Succession to the Throne of Siam is, in theory, regulated by the law ... according to which the eldest son of the queen shall have precedence over all other members of the royal family. Owing to the frequency of its violation throughout Siamese history resulting from usurpation by a powerful noble or the outcome of a struggle for supremacy amongst the surviving sons of a king, the student of Siamese history might hardly suspect the existence of such a law. (Quaritch Wales, 1931)

The ambitions and influence of the elite were the primary reason for the persistence of succession conflicts, as David Wyatt argues in his history of Thailand:

> Political conflicts in Siam tended to reflect the competition of major noble families for power more than royal preoccupations and infighting. The nobles were the real element of continuity in the system, single families continuing for as many as seven generations with a member in a ministerial position. The nobles put and kept kings on the throne, and kings maintained the substance of royal power only by carefully manipulating public appointments so as to balance the noble families against each other or by bringing in others to compete with them. Royal rule was a delicate business for high stakes. (Wyatt, 2003)

The constant efforts of elite families to increase their own position in the hierarchy could sometimes destabilize the state so severely that the whole edifice was at risk of collapsing or being conquered. In the mid sixteenth century, a period of particularly poor governance and incessant fighting over the throne led to Ayutthaya become a vassal state of the Burmese. Wyatt argues that Ayutthaya's vulnerability during this era was a direct result of the structural tensions between the monarch and the elite that caused the palace to become progressively weaker:

> The Ayutthaya kings had begun, a century earlier under King Trailok, to institutionalize the control of labour through the appointment of officials from the capital to take charge of the labor and military service owed by all freemen. This bureaucratic approach could only work, however, if the monarch could be absolutely sure of the loyalties of his chief officers. At the beginning of a dynasty's rule, this group would be composed of the new king's closest friends and allies. Over the course of several reigns, however, the close personal relations between a powerful, prosperous nobility and successive monarchs would naturally lose some of the personal quality with which they had begun, until finally one or more factions within the nobility would amass the labor and resources necessary to depose the king and begin the cycle again with a new dynasty. This process of disintegration of the institutional ties within the Ayutthaya state already had reached an advanced stage by the 1560s. (Wyatt, 2003)

During the seventeenth century, as more foreign powers set up trading outposts in Ayutthaya, the influx of outsiders further destabilized Thai politics. Foreign factions embroiled themselves in succession conflicts, hoping to win commercial and political influence by helping put their favoured candidate for monarch on the throne. This gave Ayutthayan monarchs more freedom of manoeuvre as they tried to limit the power of the old nobility. The traditional Thai elite, which controlled labour, could be played off against influential foreigners who facilitated international trade. As Wyatt explains:

> Outsiders thus were enabled not only to high official positions but also to found dynasties of royal officers who monopolized

certain state offices and played prominent political roles. Their
descendants continued in such positions into the twentieth century.
(Wyatt, 2003)

One influential aristocratic family, the Bunnag clan, was
founded by two Persian brothers who arrived in 1602 and rose to
important official positions. The wealth amassed by the Bunnags
enabled them to exert immense influence over successive royal
dynasties. The established noble families were horrified by the
ease with which foreigners could accumulate power at the royal
court. Matters came to a head after King Narai – who seized
the throne in 1656 with the help of Japanese, Patani Malay and
Persian factions – grew increasingly dependent on the services of
a Greek adventurer, Constantine Phaulkon. Phaulkon's constant
scheming, including a quixotic effort to get Narai to convert
to Catholicism and ally with France, infuriated other foreign
communities and the traditional kingmakers of the Thai elite.
In 1688, with Narai's health failing and royal succession imminent, Phaulkon's leading Thai rival at the court seized power.
Phaulkon was executed, along with Narai's sons, and the French
were driven from the kingdom. For the next century and a half,
the ability of Western countries to influence Siamese politics was
drastically curtailed.

Inevitably, the declining power of the monarchy and the increasing autonomy of the nobility set in motion another cycle of
fraying state authority. Despite efforts to edit them out of the royal
chronicles and to depict Thai kingdoms as happy and harmonious,
popular uprisings and rebellions were far more common in the
seventeenth and eighteenth centuries than the elite admitted. Chris
Baker notes that in *Khun Chang Khun Phaeng*, 'repeatedly through
the story, the king is afflicted by fear of revolt' (Baker, 2008).

Millenarian peasant uprisings

Almost all of the popular revolts by ordinary people that erupted in Thai kingdoms up to the early twentieth century took the form of millenarian or messianic movements revolving around charismatic 'holy men', drawing strength from the Buddhist tradition in which legitimacy to lead derives from religious merit and virtuous conduct, not royal blood. Traditional Buddhist doctrines preached submissive acceptance of the existing hierarchical social order and accumulation of merit that would lead to a better life in future incarnations, while radical millenarianism, by contrast, gave peasants the hope of dramatically improving their situation in this lifetime. As Shigeharu Tanabe explains:

> Hegemonic Buddhism has been able to manipulate popular consent to the karmic order of the world through a highly organized system at all social levels, and it has succeeded in fostering the popular belief that salvation comes in the other world in accordance with the accumulation of merit in this world. The manipulation of consent is continually activated by ritual communication between monks and laymen centring on the Buddhist temple, the ideological power station...
>
> Buddhist millenarianism envisages an immediate salvation by the Messiah, and the coming of a new era to be established in this world, through collective sentiment and behaviour. (Tanabe, 1984)

The ordinary people who joined these rebellions believed that a better world was about to dawn, in which their grim lives would be transformed thanks to the arrival of a truly righteous ruler. 'Though it so often ends tragically, this radical bias for hope, the conviction that the world is heading their way, is worthy of our careful attention and perhaps even our admiration', observes Scott, noting that millennial 'holy man' revolts in Southeast Asia bear 'an unmistakeable family resemblance to the expectations of other dispossessed and stigmatized peoples':

the Anabaptists of the Reformation civil wars, the cargo
cults of Melanesia, the belief of Russian serfs that the tsar
had issued a decree freeing them, the conviction among New
World slaves that a redeemer was at hand, and hundreds of
other millenarian expectations of a coming (or returning) king
or god, by no means confined to Judeo-Christian settings.
Ironically, these misreadings of the world were occasionally so
widespread and massive that they touched off rebellions that in
fact changed the odds. (Scott, 2009)

Revolts were particularly common among ethnic Lao in the
regions of Lanna and Isaan in the north and north-east of the
Ayutthayan mandala state. In 1699, a holy man named Bun Kwang
took control of the city of Nakhon Ratchasima and held out against
royal authority for more than a year. This peasant rebellion was
significant enough to remain part of recorded history, but many
others were erased from the annals.

During Chulalongkorn's reign, several millenarian peasant
uprisings roiled northern and north-eastern Thailand as the aggressively centralizing king sought to tighten his grip on the old
kingdom of Lanna and the Isaan region. A strict taxation regime
was introduced, and traditional local power structures were sup-
planted by the bureaucratic machinery of the absolutist state. This
caused multiple millenarian rebellions in Chiang Mai province
around 1889–90, Khon Kaen province in 1895, several parts of
Isaan in 1901–02, and Phrae in 1902 (Chatthip, 1984). These
followed a similar pattern to the 'holy man' revolts of previous
centuries, with peasants rallying under charismatic leaders and
declaring independence from exploitation and oppression by the
state. They were put down brutally by the Siamese authorities. As
Charles Keyes observes, these uprisings were evidence of 'a crisis
centering around political power' (Keyes, 1977). The claim that all
Thais were united in their reverence for a fatherly monarch was
plainly false. Elite hegemony could not be preserved by royalist
ideology alone – it required violence and coercion.

As the eighteenth century progressed, a growing number of ordinary Thais found ways to evade the exploitation of the state, which found itself increasingly starved of labour and wealth:

> Through much of the century, repeated royal laws and edicts had called attention to shortages of labor available to the government. It is clear that many freemen subject to annual compulsory labor service were evading their obligations. Some managed simply to avoid registration; others placed themselves under the protection of individual princes or officials.

By the 1760s, Wyatt adds, 'there was a serious labour shortage in Ayutthaya' (Wyatt, 2003). Meanwhile, another prolonged period of internecine conflict ended with the incompetent King Ekkathat seizing the throne. According to Wood,

> The new King ... was a man of poor intelligence and worthless character. In a book written only twenty-two years after his death he is described as 'void of intelligence, unsettled in spirit, fearful of sin, negligent in all his kingly duties hesitating alike to do good or evil.' He was, in short, utterly unfitted to guide his country through the perils which were destined to overwhelm it.

'Fully occupied in suppressing ... internal intrigues', adds Wood, the king 'never gave a thought to the dangers across the frontier' (Wood, 1926). According to Thai accounts, after Burmese forces finally breached the city walls, torching and demolishing the royal capital, Ekkathat fled in a small boat; he starved to death in a nearby forest ten days later, unable to fend for himself. Burmese war chronicles tell a different story, saying Ayutthaya's king was shot near the west gate of the capital as he tried to escape. Whatever the truth of its last monarch's ignominious death, 416 years after it was founded, the kingdom of Ayutthaya – fatally weakened by chronic succession conflict and inept leadership – had been obliterated.

EIGHT

'One neither walks, speaks, drinks, eats, nor cooks without some kind of ceremony'

The pleasures and privations of being king

On 10 December 1636, around a dozen drunken Dutchmen were detained by palace authorities in Ayutthaya after a picnic went disastrously wrong. The men, employees of the Dutch trading post, had taken a boat trip a short distance upriver from the city with some food and alcohol, heading for an important temple. As Jeremias Van Vliet, acting director of the Dutch outpost in Ayutthaya, wrote in an official report on the incident: 'this day of merriment ended in great sadness, because before the day was done, the entire party found itself in mortal danger.' After an altercation with monks who objected to them picnicking at the temple, some of the Dutch day-trippers went on the rampage in the surrounding countryside, insulting and assaulting several locals, including some slaves belonging to the king's younger brother. The incensed prince ordered the whole group arrested. When King Prasart Thong heard what had happened the following morning he sent guards to strip them naked, bind their hands and feet, and drag them to his palace. The king declared they would be trampled to death by elephants. Thousands of spectators turned up to watch. Frantically, Van Vliet began contacting influential officials, bribing and cajoling them to intercede to save the lives of the picnic party. Prasart Thong eventually agreed to spare them from execution, but they remained in detention, and the king placed severe restrictions on the ability of the Dutch to conduct trade. To secure the release of the prisoners and the lifting of trade restrictions, Van Vliet was obliged to sign a document taking personal responsibility for the behaviour of the Dutch community and crawl through the palace on his hands and knees to perform a ritual of apology in front of the king (Van Vliet, 2005).

When the Dutch authorities in Java learned of the episode, they were furious that Van Vliet had agreed to abase himself before Ayutthaya's king, an act they regarded as highly damaging to Dutch prestige. He was summoned to Batavia to explain himself. While waiting to learn his fate, he wrote a lengthy report on the kingdom of Ayutthaya. It was one of the most detailed and useful accounts of the early Thai state ever published, remarkable above all for its description of the terrifying rule of Prasart Thong, a usurper who had seized the throne in 1629 and who appears to have been particularly paranoid even by the standards of Thai kings, desperate to demonstrate his legitimacy and erase the stain of his status as an interloper. Van Vliet described a dystopian realm ruled by a violent and unpredictable monarch who was frequently drunk and surrounded by scheming senior officials, or 'mandarins'. 'Nobody dared to oppose the king or to resist his pride', he wrote, noting the severity of royal taboos and numerous examples of ritualized violence, including the practice of sacrificing pregnant women under the foundations of royal buildings in order to turn them into powerful guardian spirits:

> The fear of His Majesty is so great that nobody, however powerful he may be, dares to mention His name, His head or His royal crown in public, even when important affairs are being discussed. In cases when it is necessary to talk about him or to call his name, the people whisper the words respectfully in each other's ear. His Majesty is honoured and worshipped by his subjects more than a god.

By the usurped authority of the kings and by the continuous praise of the people the pride of the former kings had reached such a height that it looked as if the king was not there for the good of his community, but that the whole country and the people were for his pleasure aloneness. The kings counted their subjects so little that if palaces, towers or resting places had to be built for them, under each post which was put into the ground a pregnant woman was thrown and the more near this woman was to her time the better. For this reason there was often great misery ... during the time that palaces or towers had to be built or repaired. For as all houses in Siam are built at a certain height above the ground and stand on wooden posts many women have endured this suffering. Although this description seems to be fabulous, these executions have really taken place.

The people, who are very superstitious, believe that these women after dying turn into terrible monsters or devils, who defend not only the post below which they are thrown but the whole house against misfortune. The King usually ordered a few slaves to catch without regard all the women who were in a pregnant state. But out of the houses no women were taken unless in the streets nobody could be found. These women were brought to the queen, who treated them as if they were of high birth. After they had been there for a few days, they were (excuse these rude words) thrown into the pit with the stomach turned upwards. After this the post was put on the stomach and driven right through it.

Another passage recounts the murder of four young women, arbitrary killings that the king believed would bring him good fortune in a military campaign against the kingdom of Patani:

On leaving his palace the king swore that the four women whom he should meet first would be made an offering to the gods and that his vessels would be besmeared with the women's flesh and blood. This was done; before His Majesty was out of the town he met four young girls sitting in a boat, and on these girls he fulfilled his oath.

The senior 'mandarins' are depicted as avaricious, corrupt and status-obsessed, and living in constant fear of the bloodthirsty whims of their monarch. In this environment, the position of the

top officials was precarious and fraught with danger. The lives of
ordinary people were even worse:

> Nobody dares to show dissatisfaction about the decision of the
> king, for his life and his position would be in danger.
>
> But one cannot rely much on the favour of the king, and for
> little mistakes, sometimes even without any reason, men filling
> high positions were discharged and from being great men became
> insignificant. All the inhabitants are really the king's slaves, which
> name is an honourable title even among the greatest, as His Majesty
> is in fact the chief person and has supreme power and authority
> over the Kingdom and the life and goods of his vassals and
> subjects...
>
> A result of the king's usurped authority and distrust was that all
> the mandarins (particularly the most influential of them, who have
> a state and a position) are kept very slavishly... They are entirely
> deprived of their former freedom. Only in the public assembly
> room and in presence of and the hearing of everybody, even of the
> slaves, are the mandarins allowed to talk to each other. Should
> they not follow this rule, their life and position would be in danger.
> The father is not allowed to visit his child, nor the child its father,
> without the knowledge and consent of the king, even in cases of
> illness or death...
>
> Although the mandarins in general are slavish and have to
> appear before the king with great humility, they are very arrogant,
> proud, and haughty, especially in regard to the titles and marks
> of honour which they have received from the king. Yes, every one
> of them wants to be served, honoured and feared as if he were a
> worldly god. They usually practise great authority over those who
> are in their houses and over their slaves. Although the greater
> number have to live on their slaves, they have to keep up a certain
> state and they do not allow themselves to be addressed otherwise
> than with bent body, folded hands, and with ceremonious
> praisings. Besides this they often tyrannise their concubines
> (or small wives) and their slaves. They make them die for small
> mistakes or throw them into prison and treat them very harshly.
> For all this an excuse is very easily found for the king, and as much
> fault is imposed on the victim as their large conscience may care
> for, and in the meantime the poor victim lies smothered in his
> blood without being able to give account. In their houses, and on

the streets the mandarins are honoured like small kings among
their subjects, but coming to court they are only slaves. (Van Vliet,
1910)

Prasart Thong is also described as a sexual predator, preying
on the wives and daughters of the elite. 'The wives of the greatest mandarins (being healthy and of good appearance) were not
allowed to stay longer than 3 or 4 days outside the court of the
queen', Van Vliet wrote. 'They were brought inside the palace
under pretext that they had to greet the king. Sometimes his
Majesty himself selected the prettiest maidens and daughters of
the greatest men, and these women were given him as concubines'
(Van Vliet, 1910). Several sources from the same period also
report a massacre of 2,900 nobles and powerful officials, ordered
by Prasart Thong ostensibly because he suspected that one of
his daughters had been poisoned (Kemp, 1969). Wood described
Prasart Thong as an 'atrocious man', adding: 'His whole reign was
a series of murders' (Wood, 1926).

Of all the dangers that have troubled the Thai ruling class
over the centuries, the prospect of an unmanageable and violent
monarch like Prasart Thong gaining power has been a particularly
persistent fear. Even the most influential noble families that had
accumulated wealth and power over multiple generations could
face ruin during the reign of a rogue king they couldn't control.
As a result, the establishment has always sought to constrain
the threat that powerful kings could pose to them. The paradox
of Thai kingship is that the theatrics and rituals intended to
demonstrate the might and glory of the monarch to ordinary
people also serve to restrict royal power and mask the fact that
most of the time kings have been puppets of the ruling class, not
their masters.

European accounts of King Narai's reign later in the seventeenth century depict a king who was remarkably isolated and constrained by ritual. This was no accident. The customs and laws of the palace suited the elite, because they restricted access to the king to only the most powerful nobles, and prevented the monarch from growing too powerful. If a king followed the rules – rather than doing as he pleased like Prasart Thong – noble families could safeguard their power and prevent emergent rival factions making contact with the monarch. In an account published in 1688, France's Nicolas Gervaise described the extraordinarily regimented life of King Narai, which roughly followed the stipulations set down in King Trailok's law two centuries earlier:

> He always rose at 7 a.m. exactly; his pages washed and dressed him and he worshipped the Buddha. After breakfast he went into the council chamber and stayed there until noon. He then had his midday meal. He was then undressed and washed and was lulled to sleep by music, to be awakened at 4 p.m. His reader then came and read history to him, sometimes for three or four hours. If he was in the capital he did not go out except for a walk in his gardens unless it was a day of state ceremonial. Sometimes he visited the palace ladies and stayed with them until 8 p.m., when it was time to meet his counsellors again. He deliberated with them until midnight and then had his supper (if he had not taken it previously) and went to bed.

Intricate rituals had to be adhered to by anyone wishing to talk to the monarch. 'One neither walks, speaks, drinks, eats, nor cooks without some kind of ceremony', wrote Gervaise. Palace law prevented the king even speaking to most of his subjects:

> What constraint it must be for him that he cannot speak to a bourgeois or peasant without being obliged to elevate him to nobility! But what trouble must it be for his subjects that they may be heard only after they have satisfied certain ceremonies that must be observed when he wishes to grant them an audience. (Gervaise, 1928)

Even if people from outside the upper nobility managed to gain an audience with the king, the requirement to use the *rajasap* language to address the monarch was a further barrier to contact – not many people knew how to speak it. As Quaritch Wales noted: 'The palace language was ... an efficient means of maintaining the gulf fixed between the king and his people' (Quaritch Wales, 1931).

In this kind of environment it was hardly surprising that kings immersed themselves in their harem, and in hobbies like hunting – or warfare. Life would have been intolerable otherwise. The royal harem, adopted from ancient Hindu traditions of kingship, was a crucial institution for the elite, cementing their ties to the palace and – they hoped – guaranteeing their exalted status. The predatory behaviour of Prasart Thong had been a breach of tradition – the accepted etiquette was for noble families and top officials to give daughters as gifts to the king, establishing what Tamara Loos describes as 'a concrete and continuous connection of blood, communication, and loyalty between the monarch and powerful groups':

> Powerful elites expressed their desire to affiliate with the monarch by providing to the king their female kin. Therefore, these women represented an opportunity for their families to create and cement an enduring blood tie to the ruling house. (Loos, 2005)

The harem took up a vast area of the inner palace. Hundreds of women and girls lived there, and the only males permitted to enter were the king and his pre-adolescent sons. As Mary Louise Grow observes, this helped give the inner palace the mystique of 'appearing as if it was a heaven on earth' (Grow, 1991). The oral poem *Khun Chang Khun Phaen* contains an account of the king's harem and enviable lifestyle:

The king emperor, ruler of Ayutthaya, the great heaven, resident of
   the glittering crystal palace where masses of palace ladies,
all just of age, radiant, fair, tender, and beautiful, with figures like
   those in a painting, serviced the royal footsoles, slumbered in
   the golden palace.
When dawn streaked the sky, he woke from sleep and came to
   bathe in cool rosewater. He was adorned in splendid raiment,
and, grasping a diamond sword in his left hand, went out to
   the main audience hall to sit on the sparkling crystal throne,
   surrounded by senior officials and royal poets. (Baker, 2008)

Besides establishing blood ties between the reigning dynasty
and nobility, the harem served the interests of top officials by
keeping the king distracted and taking up a significant amount of
his time, giving them more leeway to quietly consolidate power
and minimize royal meddling. 'It would really depend almost
entirely on the personality of the individual king', wrote Quaritch
Wales, rather disapprovingly. 'A strong-minded ruler ... would
realize that the harem was a sacred institution of his country,
and would be unlikely to lapse into sensuality, but we know from
history that such was the temptation to which many a weaker
monarch succumbed' (Quaritch Wales, 1931).

When faced with monarchs they were unable to manage, the
ruling class plotted constantly to topple them. King Taksin, who
claimed the throne after the destruction of Ayutthaya, was insuf-
ficiently servile to the members of the old noble families who
escaped massacre or enslavement at the hands of the Burmese,
and this led directly to his overthrow and execution – and the
rise of the Chakri dynasty. Among the innovations introduced
by Rama I was a change to the rules of succession – an accession
council of senior princes and nobles would oversee the process,
so disputes could hopefully be managed through consensus rather
than bloodletting. This formalized the influence of the kingmakers

behind the throne. The noble families were re-establishing power, as Pasuk and Baker explain:

> The great families that survived 1767, and especially a handful personally connected to the Chakri family, rose rapidly in the new era. A few new lineages also rose through military achievement and filled the spaces left by those killed or hauled away during the wars. Some dozen great households monopolized the powerful positions in the central administration. They intermarried with one another and the Chakri family. They participated in the revival of the commercial economy. They were not obstructed by royal antagonism. Some became almost as splendid as the ruling family itself. (Pasuk and Baker, 2009a)

But family squabbles and succession struggles persisted. During the reigns of Rama I and Rama II scores of people were executed for aiding plots to seize the throne. The succession following the death of Rama II in 1824 was particularly contentious. Only one prince had celestial status in the royal family – the king's 19-year-old son Mongkut. But the candidate backed by the noble families – and the Bunnag clan in particular – was Rama II's 37-year-old eldest son, whose mother had been a concubine rather than a queen. Predictably, the rules of succession were overlooked and the elite's preferred candidate became king. Mongkut was concerned enough about his safety to remain in the monkhood throughout Rama III's twenty-seven-year reign. When the king died, the succession was contested once again, but this time Mongkut had secured the support of the nobility and was chosen as Rama IV.

Although a celebrated figure in Thai history, Mongkut was a remarkably weak monarch who exemplified the paradoxes of Siamese kingship. As historian Kullada Kesbonchoo Mead says, 'he remained a client of the great nobles throughout his reign'

(Kullada, 2004). He was a figurehead, living in splendour but isolated. Inevitably, he spent considerable time in the harem. After living the celibate life of a monk until he became king at the age of 46, Mongkut fathered 82 children by 35 women during his 17-year reign.

Chulalongkorn had even less power than his father when he became Rama V. Besides putting him on the throne, the nobles had also selected a rival prince as *uparaja* or deputy king. Tensions between the two of them led to the 'Front Palace crisis' of December 1874, an apparent plot by the *uparaja* and his supporters to seize the throne. But Chulalongkorn proved to be a far more formidable figure than the ruling oligarchy had anticipated. He was another aggressively centralizing monarch, and the reforms he pushed through during his reign were intended not only to prevent direct colonization by the British but also to break the power of the old elite and assert the primacy of the palace. As Kullada argues, 'wresting control over the growing revenues from the great nobles was the main feature of state building in the second half of the 19th century' (Kullada, 2004). Chulalongkorn also abolished the position of *uparaja* when the incumbent died, introducing the position of crown prince in its place. It was another attempt to regularize royal succession and, as Noel Battye says, prevent it being influenced by 'princely grasping, ministerial manipulation and foreign intervention' (Battye, 1974).

Chulalongkorn's reforms dramatically changed the composition of the country's elite but did not end feuding over the royal succession. His son Vajiravudh, King Rama VI, further modified the fifteeenth-century palace law on succession in 1924, ostensibly to clarify an ambiguity that had arisen because of the large number of celestial princes Chulalongkorn had fathered with various queens. The real reason was that he loathed the eldest *chao fa* in the royal family, his half-brother Paribatra, and wanted to elevate the succession prospects of his full brothers, who were born to a more senior queen. Upon his death the following year, the ineffectual Prajadhipok, second youngest of Chulalongkorn's seventy-seven children, became Rama VII thanks to Vajiravudh's tinkering with the rules. Prajadhipok had never expected to be king and was so overwhelmed by the prospect that he tried to pass the crown to Paribatra instead (Stowe, 1991). The offer was rebuffed, but the senior princes dominated the younger king throughout his reign.

Prajadhipok agonized over the entangled problems of royal succession and demands for democracy. The end of royal polygamy as the Thai elite scrambled to show themselves to be 'civilized' by Western standards had dramatically reduced the pool of potential candidates for kingship, raising the risk that incompetent or maverick monarchs would inherit the throne. As Prajadhipok wrote to US adviser Francis Sayre in 1926:

> As you well know, the king has absolute power in everything. This principle is very good and very suitable for the country, *as long as we have a good king*. If the king is really an elected king, it is probable that he would be a fairly good king.
> But this idea of election is really a theoretical one. The kings of Siam are really hereditary, with a very limited possibility of choice. Such being the case, it is not at all certain that we shall always have a good king. The absolute power may become a positive danger to the country.
> Besides this … in olden days the actions of the king were hardly ever questioned… The king was really respected and his words were really laws… In the reign which has just ended, things got much worse… Every official is more or less suspected of embezzlement or nepotism. Fortunately the princes were still respected as being on the whole honest folks. What was very

regrettable was that the court was heartily detested and in the later years was on the verge of being ridiculed. The birth of free press aggravated matters still more.

The position of king has become one of great difficulty. The movements of opinion in this country give a sure sign that the days of autocratic rulership are numbered. The position of the king must be made more secure if this dynasty is going to last. Some kind of guarantee must be found against an unwise king. (Batson, 1974)

Prajadhipok had no children, and refused to name a successor when he abdicated in 1935. By now a new elite were in the ascendant – the military and civilian revolutionaries of 1932 – but the political calculus was the same as throughout Thai history. The country's new rulers wanted a monarch they could control and who would legitimize their dominance. There were no surviving celestial princes in Prajadhipok's bloodline, and had the laws of succession been followed the throne should have been inherited by the hawkish Paribatra, exiled in Java. Second in line was the 12-year-old Prince Varananda, who had been adopted by Prajadhipok and lived with him in England. Both these candidates were unacceptable to the government and so – as usual – the rules were ignored and the 9-year-old Ananda Mahidol was proclaimed Rama VIII instead. His dynastic claim was extremely weak, but he was just what they wanted – an absentee boy king from outside the royalist network.

When Ananda's sudden and violent death propelled Bhumibol onto the throne, the royal succession appeared straightforward and uncontested – a rare phenomenon in Thai history. But this was an illusion. An unacknowledged story of dark family secrets, palace feuds and succession struggles runs right through Bhumibol's long reign. It provides the key to understanding Thailand's twenty-first-century crisis.

NINE

'I cannot afford to die'
The tragedy of King Bhumibol

Bhumibol would never have become king of Thailand if he and
his mother had told the truth about Ananda's death. In the weeks
after the shooting, the government began to discover compelling
evidence that Rama VIII had not committed suicide as they had
assumed. Bhumibol had shot his brother through the head, probably by mistake, pulling the trigger while playing with Ananda,
not realizing that the Colt 45 was loaded (Marshall, 2013). Had
Bhumibol and Sangwan admitted what had happened, the heir
presumptive Prince Chumbhot – son of the hawkishly royalist
Paribatra, who had died in exile in Java in 1944 – would have
become monarch instead.

Even after they realized the truth, Pridi's government covered
up what happened. It suited them to have a weak monarch on the
throne; the prospect of the assertive Chumbhot becoming king
was much more worrying. The royalists and Phibun's military
faction also conspired to conceal the truth, exploiting the regicide
to smear Pridi and provide the pretext for their coup in 1947. But
after allying with the military to overthrow Pridi, the royalists
became increasingly unhappy with Bhumibol. They wanted a
strong king who could rally support for the royalist cause. Bhumibol was indecisive, unassertive and languishing in Lausanne, deep
in depression. In 1948, leaders of the royalist Democrat Party

hatched a plan to reveal that Bhumibol had killed his brother, to force him to abdicate (Marshall, 2013). Phibun's military faction, like Pridi's progressives, wanted to keep Bhumibol on the throne precisely because he was weak and appeared harmless. The explosive secret of his killing of Ananda could be used to keep him under control – as Roger Kershaw observes, it left Bhumibol vulnerable to 'blackmailing insinuation' (Kershaw, 2001). Realizing the royalists wanted to topple Bhumibol and replace him with Chumbhot, Phibun foiled the plot by ousting the Democrat Party and seizing power in April 1948. Meanwhile, a sensational show trial began of two palace pages and a former royal secretary falsely accused of plotting to murder Ananda on behalf of Pridi. As so often before in Thai history, a dominant elite faction was trying to keep a pliant monarch on the throne, while rival factions sought to replace the king with an alternative candidate who could better serve their interests.

After he finally returned in 1951 to formally take up his duties, Bhumibol was ignored by Thailand's military rulers. He later told the *New York Times*: 'When I'd open my mouth and suggest something, they'd say: "Your Majesty, you don't know anything." So I shut my mouth. I know things, but I shut my mouth. They don't want me to speak, so I don't speak' (Crosette, 1989). Kobkua describes Bhumibol during this period as 'a non-entity ruler in the affairs of the nation' and a mere 'figurehead whose duty it was to symbolize the nation through parts played in various religious and traditional rites and ceremonies' (Kobkua, 2003). The king tried to assert his influence during disputes with the junta by threatening to abdicate, but they were able to respond with a threat of their own – revealing the truth about the death of his brother. Unwilling to live in the Grand Palace following the trauma of 1946, Bhumibol made Chitralada Palace his Bangkok home, and spent months of each year at 'Far from Worries' villa in Hua Hin. His choice of residences symbolized royal weakness – there was no reigning monarch in the Grand Palace. In July 1952, Sirikit gave birth to a son – the first celestial prince to be born since Chulalongkorn's reign. He was given a mighty name – Vajiralongkorn, 'possessor of the thunderbolt' – but he seemed destined to inherit a powerless throne.

In 1955, after three trials that had dragged on since 1948, police chief Phao Sriyanond oversaw the execution of the three scapegoats in the regicide case. Phibun, who wanted to prevent the case being closed to allow him to use it for leverage against the royalists, applied for a royal pardon for the accused men three times after they were sentenced to death. Bhumibol rejected the requests (Sulak, 2000). *Time* magazine described the executions, and noted the widespread belief that the case had not been solved at all:

> At 5 o'clock one morning last week, fortified with a final bottle of orange squash apiece, the three were led into the execution pavilion at Bangkwang Prison. Their hands were clasped together in the traditional Buddhist greeting and lashed to an upright pole. In each upraised hand, prison guards placed a ceremonial candle, joss sticks and a garland of small, pink Siamese orchids. Then a dark blue curtain was dropped behind each victim and the executioner fired a burst from his machine gun... At last the execution was done, the closet was tidy, and only one question remained unanswered: Who killed King Ananda? (*Time*, 1955)

Justice had been done – officially, at least – and Bhumibol's guilt could remain hidden, but at the cost of allowing three innocent men to die. Kershaw argues the king had little choice: 'It might be said in defence of King Bhumibol in relation to the execution of innocent men that the situation had become very difficult for him because he had already begun to pit his prerogative against the ruling military clique over the coup-legitimizing Constitution of 1951–52' (Kershaw, 2001). In fact, he could certainly have saved their lives if he wanted. He chose not to. The secret still haunts Thailand's monarchy.

The executions made Bhumibol's position more secure, and, boosted by his alliance with the army following Sarit's coup of 1957, he began gradually restoring the influence of the palace. The emergent coalition of monarchy, the old royalist establishment, the ethnic Chinese capitalist elite and the military was cemented by the increasingly wealthy Crown Property Bureau, which bound the oligarchy together in a web of business deals and investments. The role of the CPB was strikingly similar to the royal harem in previous centuries, forging links among the disparate elements of the ruling class. Business relationships had replaced blood relationships, but the principle remained the same. Intermarriage among members of the extended royal family, the old noble clans, the tycoon class and the military elite also continued to play an important part in consolidating the oligarchy.

But, as always, intra-elite conflict and rivalry remained a highly destabilizing factor in Thai politics, despite the economic and sexual ties that wove the ruling class together. Feuding and squabbles even extended into Bhumibol's immediate family, and by the 1970s the relationship between the king and queen had grown fractious. Much of the friction revolved around Vajiralongkorn. As the prince grew up, Bhumibol became increasingly dismayed by his son's personality and behaviour, although Sirikit doted on her boy. Handley says that by the beginning of the 1970s, Vajiralong-korn 'had become a disagreeable young man lacking any of the intellect, charm, curiosity, or diplomatic skills of his parents' and who 'treated aides with little respect and women as objects, using his power to get them to sleep with him' (Handley, 2006a). When he turned 20 in 1972, Vajiralongkorn was formally designated heir to the throne. But he was already remarkably unpopular among Thais, who mocked and scorned him in private conversations. Far more admired was the prince's younger sister Sirindhorn, an apparently amiable and unpretentious young woman whom many ordinary Thais adored.

Bhumibol and Sirikit were also divided over the appropriate political role of the palace. Both were firm believers in elite rule and a politically influential monarchy, but Bhumibol favoured a more consensual and subtle approach while the queen wanted aggressive action to crush their perceived enemies. Sirikit believed she was a reincarnation of the sixteenth-century Queen Suriyothai, who – according to legend – had ridden into battle on elephant back disguised as a man to defend her husband and save Ayutthaya. As semi-official royal biographer William Stevenson wrote:

> Sirikit still returned in her dreams to what she believed was her earlier incarnation as a warrior queen. She consulted her own informants, who were full of stories about plots to bring down her husband. She shot at cardboard targets, saying bluntly that Buddha sanctioned the destruction of evil. Her targets represented live enemies… Photographs show her with lustrous black hair tied back, bracing herself against the sandbags, her long slim fingers supporting the rifle or curled around the trigger. She looks like a legendary Siamese woman warrior with a white ribbon around her head. (Stevenson, 1999)

Marital discord in the palace and widespread contempt for Vajilongkorn fuelled the incendiary political atmosphere in Thailand in the mid-1970s and the explosion of violence in October 1976. The pretext for the Thammasat massacre was a play staged

by students in the campus two days earlier – newspapers published front-page photographs of a mock hanging that was part
of the drama, and rightists alleged it was intended to depict the
execution of the crown prince, a claim those involved in the play
have always denied (Thongchai, 2002). Whatever the truth, it
was exploited by the far right to unleash an orgy of murder and
brutality that shocked the world. Vajiralongkorn became more
feared and hated than ever.

Widespread dread of the prospect that Vajiralongkorn could
one day become king drew on historic fears of the terror wrought
by violent monarchs, and the traditional belief that the world was
on the brink of a dark age, or *kaliyug*. Many Thais came to believe
that Vajiralongkorn's reign would be this blighted era, and anxiety
was stoked by an old prophecy that the monarchy would collapse
after the ninth Chakri reign. After two decades of relentless
royalist propaganda, it was widely assumed that the downfall of
the monarchy would spell catastrophe for the country. The elite
had particular reason for angst about Vajiralongkorn: unlike the
generally pliable Bhumibol, whom they trusted to protect their
interests and preserve the sacred aura of the monarchy, the crown
prince was volatile and belligerent. They feared he could become
a dangerous rogue monarch like Prasart Thong, one whose whims
and rages could unravel generations of accumulated wealth and
power for those unlucky enough to anger him. They were further
scandalized and enraged by Vajiralongkorn's habit of preying on
their daughters. The prince became notorious for summoning
attractive high-born young women to his palace. The extent to
which it happened remains unknown, but it was a source of
profound anger and anxiety among the elite, many of whom sent
their daughters for education overseas to escape his attentions.

In January 1977, pressured by the queen, who wanted to ensure her own branch of the royal family would predominate, Vajiralongkorn married Soamsawali, a cousin from Sirikit's bloodline. The marriage was a disaster. The prince was regularly seen in the company of wealthy strongmen who made their fortunes in the nexus of crime, politics and business. Thais began to refer to him derisively as 'Sia-O', a combination of the word for a Chinese–Thai gangster and the sixth syllable of his royal title. Frustrated by his son's behaviour, in December 1977 the king elevated Sirindhorn to the status of potential heir to the throne too. Officials characterized this as a precaution in case anything happened to Vajiralongkorn and claimed it did not cast the prince's status into doubt, but it generated significant ambiguity, which still remains. Support for Sirindhorn to be the next monarch became remarkably widespread and surprisingly openly expressed. Although the palace succession law specified that only males could accede to the throne, Thai constitutions began specifying that a woman could be nominated as monarch – a clear sign that much of the elite preferred Sirindhorn too. By the 1980s there was intense mutual animosity between Vajiralongkorn and most of Thailand's establishment, who wanted Bhumibol to remain on the throne as long as possible and overwhelmingly favoured Sirindhorn to be the next monarch when he died.

During 1978, the prince abandoned his wife and moved in with Yuwathida Pholprasert, a nightclub hostess and aspiring actress. Soamsawali bore Vajiralongkorn a daughter in late 1978, and in 1979 Yuwathida gave birth to a son, Vajiralongkorn's first male heir. Over the next decade, Yuwathida was to bear him four more children. Sirikit remained the prince's staunchest supporter, but used a visit to the United States in 1981 to publicly rebuke

Vajiralongkorn for his womanizing, declaring at a news conference in Texas:

> My son the crown prince is a little bit of a Don Juan. He is a good student, a good boy, but women find him interesting and he finds women even more interesting... If the people of Thailand do not approve of the behaviour of my son, then he would either have to change his behaviour or resign from the royal family. (Handley, 2006a)

But during the 1980s, the queen's own behaviour was causing a worsening crisis. She had asserted herself as the dominant personality in the palace, and her unconcealed political activism was causing mounting discontent. 'The Queen, her entourage of generals and a few civilian advisers are effectively governing Thailand today through regular dinners at which the King does not participate', reported *The Times* (Watts, 1983). Meanwhile, Sirikit's open infatuation with one of her military aides, Narongdej Nandha-phothidej, became increasingly embarrassing to the elite, and in 1984 he was sent to the United States as a military attaché. In May 1985, he died after a game of tennis. The official explanation was that the 38-year-old colonel had suffered a heart attack, but many Thais – including Sirikit herself – suspected something more sinister. Her very public grief over the colonel's death spiralled into a breakdown, and at the end of 1985 she vanished from view for months (Handley, 2006a). With public disquiet growing, the royal couple's youngest daughter, Princess Chulabhorn, was enlisted to calm anxiety in a televised interview:

> We all work for his majesty because of our loyalty towards him. Nobody in our family wants popularity for themselves. Everybody is sharing the work and we work as a team... But again, there are people who say that our family is divided into two sides, which is not true at all. (McBeth, 1986)

In fact, it was all too true. The family was divided, and Bhumibol and Sirikit's marriage was effectively over. They lived separate lives for the next two decades, a rival royal court of ultra-right-wing politics and all-night dinner dances developing around Sirikit.

As his marriage collapsed, Bhumibol shocked the nation on his 59th birthday in 1986 by hinting he would soon step aside to make way for Vajiralongkorn. As usual, he used oblique language to hint at his intentions, drawing on the water symbolism that had always been central to the theology of Thai kingship:

> The water of the Chao Phraya must flow on, and the water that flows on will be replaced. In our lifetime, we just perform our duties. When we retire, somebody else will replace us...
>
> One cannot stick to a single task forever. One day we will grow old and die.

Palace officials confirmed Bhumibol planned to retire to a monastery some time after he turned 60 – his fifth cycle birthday in Buddhist terms – and after another important anniversary in July 1988 when he would become the longest reigning monarch in Thai history. Tongnoi Tongyai, a semi-official spokesman for Bhumibol, set out the likely scenario:

> The king will never abdicate, if by abdication you mean leaving his responsibilities behind and retiring... Once his majesty sees the crown prince reaching a more mature age and ready to take over all the royal functions, he may enter a monastery... It does not mean that he will remain a monk. The important thing is that he will continue to be there, behind the throne, and help his son solve any problems. (Handley, 1986a)

In September 1987, Vajiralongjorn was sent on a state visit to Japan. It was a chance to demonstrate he possessed the maturity and gravitas to become king. Given the stakes, things could hardly have turned out worse. The prince was enraged by several perceived insults, as the *New York Times* reported:

A Japanese chauffeur driving the Thai Prince's car apparently stopped at a motorway tollbooth to relieve himself – Japanese officials say the man felt ill and had to be replaced. On other occasions, the Prince was said to have been given an inappropriate chair to sit on and to have been forced to reach down to the floor to pick up a cord to unveil a memorial. The prince came home three days earlier than scheduled, leaving a diplomatic crisis in his wake. (Crosette, 1987)

Bhumibol's planned abdication made some sense in terms of the long-term preservation of the monarchy, but there was panic among much of the establishment. Sukhumband Paribatra, a senior member of the royal family whose status gave him some degree of protection, took the lead in publicly voicing elite fears. He explained the establishment's worries in the *Far Eastern Economic Review* in January 1988:

Given the monarchy's role in Thailand's political and economic development, as well as its place in the hearts and minds of the populace, any uncertainty regarding the future of the monarch inevitably causes a great deal of apprehension. Doubts continue to be expressed, mostly in private but now increasingly in the open, about the crown prince's capacity to evoke the kind of intense political loyalty from the people and the major domestic political groupings that his father is able to do. Doubts also persist as to whether the crown prince can match his father's subtle and mediatory role in politics. (Sukhumband, 1988)

Behind the scenes other leading figures, particularly Prem, were also actively trying to sabotage the plan. Soon afterwards, palace officials spread word that Bhumibol would not be abdicating after all. No reason was ever given. The ruling class had succeeded in keeping Vajiralongkorn off the throne, for the moment at least.

It was an indication of where power really lay in Thailand – Bhumibol was officially venerated, but his ability to act

independently of the elite was extremely limited. Socially isolated, and often seemingly adrift from reality, the king was a
relatively weak figure in the 'network monarchy' – just as most
Thai monarchs had been throughout history. He was an ideal
king for the ruling class – pliable, distant, but beloved by many
ordinary people for his perceived goodness. The elite used the
king's sacred aura to legitimize their supremacy, and to convince
inferiors in the network that their instructions were imbued with
royal authority. Once 'king's men' like Prem managed to cloak
themselves in royal *barami*, they had considerable latitude to
use the network to advance their own interests. Nobody knows
whether instructions genuinely come from the king. As the US
embassy observed in a secret cable,

> Many figures in the various circles attempt to appropriate the
> charisma of the King and prestige of the royal institution for their
> own purposes without any official remit, a process known in Thai
> as 'ang barami.' ... Even Thai relatively close to royal principals
> treat purported wishes conveyed by other royal associates
> with caution, given the tradition of self-serving 'ang barami.'
> (09BANGKOK2967)

During the 1990s, Vajiralongkorn's antics continued to appal
the establishment. In 1996, when Japanese prime minister Ryutaro
Hashimoto arrived for a summit, his 747 was blocked on the
runway for twenty minutes, as it taxied towards the red carpet,
by three F-5 fighter jets, one of them piloted by the prince. This
was Vajiralongkorn's revenge for the disrespect he believed he
was shown during his visit to Japan nine years previously. A
few months later, as Thailand prepared for Bhumibol's Golden
Jubilee, the crown prince caused a scandal that transfixed the
nation, banishing his second wife Yuwathida from his palace
and from Thailand. Besides the terrible publicity it attracted,

Vajiralongkorn's melodramatic marriage breakdown dealt a severe blow to his succession prospects, because he also disowned and expelled the four sons Yuwathida had borne him. The crown prince was left with no legitimate male heir.

The issue of royal succession was central to the promulgation of the reformist 'People's Constitution' of 1997. The two foremost proponents of reform, Anand Panyarachun and Prawase Wasi, were surprisingly explicit that a key motivation behind the new charter was the need to create a constitutional framework that could keep Vajiralongkorn in check. The new constitution was designed to allow the oligarchy to defend and preserve their exalted position and influence even if the crown prince became king. But most of the elite convinced themselves it would never happen. They thought that sooner or later he would so something so egregiously unacceptable it would ruin his succession prospects. They also believed that Bhumibol shared the widespread concern about his wayward son and would make Sirindhorn his heir instead at the opportune moment. The clearest signal of this was an extraordinary book by Canadian author William Stevenson, who spent several years in Bangkok after being enlisted by the king and granted unprecedented access to write a semi-official biography. *The Revolutionary King* was published in 1999 to derision from academics – it was riddled with basic errors and as a work of serious history was a risible failure. But as an insight into the mindset of the palace inner circle it was invaluable. Several passages hinted at the prince's notoriety as a sexual predator:

> 'Why is he giving you the Evil Eye?' a lovely young member of the Royal Household Bureau asked me, when [Vajiralongkorn] presided over the casting of Buddha images. I suggested he was looking at her, not me. She shivered: 'I hope not – it's fatal for a woman.' ...

'Perfection was too much to ask from a boy who was Heir Apparent', lamented an American-educated noblewoman. 'Look at these pictures of him in court dress-up! If he had to submit to old customs, then he might as well go all the way, have all the women he wanted, and behave like the earlier kings.'

Towards the end of the book, Stevenson evokes an atmosphere of impending doom as Bhumibol's reign approaches its end, and suggests the king favours Sirindhorn to succeed him:

'I cannot afford to die', he joked. All he had worked toward would be in jeopardy the very moment it might seem that his life was running out. The Crown Prince would never allow Crown Princess Sirindhorn to inherit the throne. She had upset her mother long ago when she decided she would never marry. The question of how much longer the king had to live was endlessly debated. Those who planned to monopolise political power could not afford to ignore the future of the Crown Princess. Even if she remained a virgin and even if there was no chance of her bearing an heir to the throne, provision had been made by the king for her to succeed him. And a majority of the people were so devoted to her that they would readily welcome her as the next monarch, however startling an innovation this might be. (Stevenson, 1999)

In mid-2000, after passing two more milestones – his sixth cycle 72nd birthday and his overtaking of Rama I to become the oldest king in Thai history – Bhumibol made another attempt to retire. This time, instead of formally abdicating, he sought instead to take a step back from his royal duties. Leaving behind the smog and stifling intrigue of Bangkok, and escaping the company of constantly watchful courtiers and his estranged queen, he decamped to 'Far from Worries' palace by the seaside in Hua Hin, where he hoped to spend the twilight of his life in relative peace.

PART IV

Crisis and confrontation

TEN

'Living in horrifying times'
Twilight of the oligarchy

About an hour after midnight on 21 March 2006, a 27-year-old man stepped onto the plinth of the ornate spirit house of the Erawan Shrine at the Ratchaprasong intersection and began battering the revered statue of the Hindu god Brahma with a hammer. It was covered with gold leaf but made of hollow plaster, and shattered easily. Two street sweepers, one of them wielding a metal bar, set upon the vandal. He died on the sidewalk near the shrine, with a four-inch blunt trauma wound to his head, severe contusions across his back, and blood oozing from his mouth. He carried no identification. A few hours later, 51-year-old Sayant Pakdeepol arrived at the local Lumphini police station after hearing on the radio what had happened and fearing the worst. He identified the corpse as his son Thanakorn, who had a history of mental illness, and had stormed out of their house nearby around midnight. 'I want to ask them why they had to beat him to death', Sayant said later. 'I see no reason why they had to go that far' (*The Nation*, 2006a).

The destruction of the statue shocked Thailand. The shrine was erected in 1956 to appease spirits believed to be enraged by the disturbance of their territory three years earlier when workmen began digging up the soil to build a hotel. Several people were injured in accidents at the construction site, and after a ship carrying a cargo of marble for the hotel lobby sank during the voyage from Italy in 1955, workmen walked out. Union officials consulted a noted astrologer, who advised them to erect a statue of Brahma. Once it was in place, the hotel was built without further problems, and the shrine quickly acquired a reputation as a place where prayers could be answered. The statue of Brahma came to be regarded as the capital's guardian deity. Its desecration fuelled an extraordinary mood of hysteria, particularly among the elite. Venerable elder statesmen had been warning for months that the country was in the grip of an unprecedented crisis. Tens of thousands of Thais were joining regular mass demonstrations in the capital, convinced that the monarchy and the kingdom were in danger. As Charles Keyes observes, the attack on the statue was widely interpreted as 'an omen related to the ongoing political crisis' (Keyes, 2006). An apocalyptic column in *The Nation* repeated an old prophecy attributed to King Narai that had predicted the destruction of Ayutthaya, and warned that modern Thailand too was on the brink of catastrophe. It blamed the leadership of Thaksin Shinawatra for dragging the country to ruin:

> The Thaksin Era, characterised by unfettered capitalism and greedy economic growth, has also been beset by bad omens. They manifest themselves in different forms, symbols and natural disasters. If a leader does not practise virtue and learning is absent among the populace, society will head into a series of crises. (*The Nation*, 2006b)

The article went on to accuse Thaksin of bringing a host of calamities upon Thailand, including the SARS virus, avian influenza and the devastating Indian Ocean tsunami of 2004. A few months later, royalist grandee Anand Panyarachun added further prognostications of doom, claiming Thailand was more divided than ever in its history. 'Thai society is now polarized by strong hatred', he warned in a speech. 'If this condition is allowed to continue, we will be living in horrifying times.'

'So why all the angst?' asked US ambassador Boyce in a cable, later obtained by WikiLeaks:

> Part of it is just that people tend to forget how bad the bad times were. But part of it may stem from the way politics and Thai society have changed in just a few years. Politics tended to be a game mostly for the elite to play. In the wake of the 1992 demonstrations that toppled the dictatorship, the 'People's Constitution' of 1997, the broader access to media brought by rising prosperity, and the populist policies of PM Thaksin – who staked his electoral success on maintaining the support of the long-disregarded rural population – politics has been, well, democratized. Within Thai society, being 'krengjai' (modest, self-effacing) is no longer such a highly prized virtue; citizens more often see the importance of demanding their rights. A much broader segment of the population feels that they have a real stake in the outcome of the political battles in Bangkok, and they are prepared to assert themselves. (06BANGKOK5429)

Beneath Thailand's superficial modernity and democracy, the skeleton of the old royalist power structure still extended throughout society. Even into the twenty-first century, an oligarchy of tycoons, bureaucrats and generals maintained immense extra-constitutional political influence. As Anderson argues, Thailand was effectively controlled by 'clusters of interlocking families, whose children go to the same schools, whose businesses are interconnected, who marry among themselves, and share a common set of values and interests' (Anderson, 2012).

The ruling class had grown and its composition had changed over the centuries, but the old *sakdina* culture of patronage and corruption had never been swept away, just overlaid by institutional and capitalist relationships that masked the persistence of older forms of power. A millennium of elite domination had even fused social inequality into the language. 'Thai linguistic structure is such that it is impossible to address a person without referring to social status', observes Hans-Dieter Bechstedt (1991), and, as Jeremy Kemp notes, 'It is worth emphasizing that this is a system in which, conceptually speaking, there are no equals' (Kemp, 1984). Englehart points out that even identical twins in Thailand 'refer to each other as elder or younger sibling ... depending on which exited the birth canal first' (Englehart, 2001). Enforced reverence of the monarchy was still used as the ideological basis for elite rule, and the palace still bonded the establishment together, using the vast wealth of the Crown Property Bureau to preserve the economic dominance of the oligarchy. During the first decade of the twenty-first century, the value of the CPB's assets had grown to at least $30 billion by the most conservative informed estimates (Porphant, 2008; Grossman and Faulder, 2011). Bhumibol was the wealthiest monarch in the world. To defend their dominance, the elite still relied upon propaganda and coercion.

But the balance of power was shifting. Thailand remained an inherently unequal society but enough wealth had trickled down to the poor to transform their lives. As anthropologist Andrew Walker notes, 'peasants in Thailand are, for the most part, no longer poor':

> They are now middle-income peasants. They are not necessarily well-off, nor do they enjoy the consumer comforts of the urban middle class, but dramatic improvements in the rural standard of living have raised most of them well above the water level of outright livelihood failure. In most areas of rural Thailand, the primary livelihood challenges have moved away from the classic low-income challenges of food security and subsistence survival to the middle-income challenges of diversification and productivity improvement. (Walker, 2012)

Thai villages were no longer the insular communities they had been in the past. The education system remained abysmal after more than a century of unfulfilled elite promises to fix it, but rural Thais had far greater contact with the world beyond the village and were better able to educate themselves. Old ideologies that required rural ignorance and passivity were becoming harder to sustain, and the inequality and exploitation that pervaded Thai society were more difficult to conceal.

The urban middle classes had become much wealthier too, and increasingly identified themselves with the elite rather than the people, jealously protective of their privileged niche in the social hierarchy. Anderson describes them as generally 'timid, selfish, uncultured, consumerist, and without any decent vision of the future of the country' (Anderson, 2012). They had overwhelmingly adopted a moralistic political philosophy which demanded clean government – a valid aspiration, but undermined by a tendency to blame corruption on the bad electoral choices of the poor rather than forming a more sophisticated understanding of systemic governance problems.

Atop the social pyramid, the elite were comfortable with the growing wealth of the middle classes, which created a rapidly expanding domestic market for the kingdom's leading conglomerates. But they were alarmed by the increasing incomes and assertiveness of the poor, which threatened the establishment's political dominance and the supply of cheap labour their businesses were built on. They were haunted, too, by fears of what would happen when Bhumibol died. Decades of animosity between Vajiralongkorn and the traditional establishment had hardened into vicious mutual loathing. The ruling class believed that if the crown prince became Rama X, he would seek revenge for their failure to respect him and their efforts to sabotage his succession prospects, removing royal patronage from the grandees of the traditional establishment and promoting a new elite in their place. It was not just political power and social prestige that were at stake – if Vajiralongkorn inherited the throne he would also gain control of the massive fortune of the Crown Property Bureau, and could divert funds away from the businesses of the old elite, eviscerating their economic supremacy.

These tensions had been building long before Bhumibol went into seclusion by the seaside at the start of the twenty-first century. The old monarch had grown increasingly troubled by the evolution of rural society away from the idealized vision of obedient peasants contentedly growing their crops. In the 1990s he began propounding what he called the 'New Theory', also known as 'sufficiency economy' philosophy. It was not really a theory, just a set of homilies about the importance of following a 'middle way', being wise and ethical, and avoiding excessive greed. But it had important implications for the poor. 'According to the king's theory, rural communities should prioritize subsistence production and localized exchange in order to develop sustainable livelihoods that are not overly exposed to the hazardous excesses of the market', explains Walker (2012). Thailand's peasants were instructed to seek only modest growth in income and maintain their traditional way of life, rather than actively pursuing all available avenues to improve their lives. It was a conservative ideology that sought to restore Thailand to a mythical past. When the economy was ravaged after the 1997 collapse of the baht, royalists hailed Bhumibol's foresight, failing to mention the monarchy's immense wealth and the fact that the Crown Property Bureau had pursued an aggressive overleveraged growth strategy that nearly bankrupted it.

Bhumibol's homilies on moderation and avoidance of greed were not only intended for the poor; he was also sending a message to Vajiralongkorn. The king was devastated by his son's profligacy and lack of Buddhist morality, and used public sermonizing to send private messages to the prince. In 1988, following his abandoned abdication, Bhumibol completed work on a version of the story of Mahajanaka, one of the *Jataka* tales about past incarnations of the Buddha. Published in 1996 to mark Bhumibol's Golden Jubilee, the book was intended as an allegory of his reign. In his preface, Bhumibol explained that he had made a change to the original version of the story, in which Mahajanaka achieves enlightenment after realizing earthly possessions bring nothing but sorrow, gives up his kingdom and his wife, and disappears into the wilderness to be a wandering monk. In Bhumibol's version, the enlightened king is unable to retire, due to the ignorance of his people:

> From the Viceroy down to the elephant mahouts and the horse handlers, and up from the horse handlers to the Viceroy, and especially the courtiers are all ignorant. They lack not only technical knowledge but also common knowledge, i.e. common sense: they do not even know what is good for them. They like mangoes, but they destroy the good mango tree. (Bhumibol, 1997)

It was an obvious rebuke to his subjects, and his son – their avarice and ignorance had forced him to abandon his retirement plans. The king also tried to restrict Vajiralongkorn's income to force the prince to start behaving better.

After finally attempting semi-retirement in 2000, Bhumibol's main project was writing another book, about his favourite dog. Published in 2002 and illustrated with several photographs of the king in a bathrobe and slippers with his brood of pet mongrels,

The Story of Tongdaeng became the best-selling book in Thai history. Its message was that Bhumibol's dog was an example for everybody to follow:

> Tongdaeng is a respectful dog with proper manners; she is humble and knows protocol. She would always sit lower than the King; even when he pulls her up to embrace her, Tongdaeng would lower herself down on the floor, her ears in a respectful drooping position, as if she would say, 'I don't dare'. (Bhumibol, 2002)

The moral of the story for Thais, and especially Vajiralongkorn, was clear. Bhumibol wanted loyal subjects and a respectful, obedient son. In the meantime, he would have to make do with Tongdaeng.

Vajiralongkorn did not react to these sermons as his father had hoped. In November 2000, showing scant regard for sufficiency economy philosophy, the crown prince ordered 350 parcels of Thai food, including pork balls, duck and prawns, from the Thai Kingdom restaurant in Stratford-upon-Avon, more than 5,000 miles from Bangkok. Staff from the Thai embassy in London had to collect the food and put it on a Thai Airways flight. Vajiralongkorn had eaten at the restaurant during a visit to Britain, and had apparently enjoyed the food enough to want a takeaway flown to Bangkok. 'It may seem a long way to fly food, but I suppose that what the prince likes, he gets', the restaurant's English owner told journalists. 'If he's happy, everybody else is happy. It's a great honour, especially for the staff. They are gobsmacked' (Branigan, 2000). Meanwhile, as Bhumibol began taking Tongdaeng with him on all his public engagements, Vajiralongkorn started doing the same with a fluffy white poodle called Foo Foo, who was always impeccably dressed in a variety of military and civilian outfits. In 2007, Boyce reported that Foo Foo had attended a gala dinner 'dressed in formal evening attire complete with paw mitts' and had been given the rank of Air Chief Marshal (07BANGKOK5839). The prince clearly revelled in the appalled reaction his antics provoked from the establishment.

The catalyst for Thailand's social and succession struggles to erupt into crisis was the political rise of Thaksin Shinawatra. Scion of a wealthy provincial Chinese Thai clan from Chiang Mai, Thaksin had sought to make a fortune via his family's connections and senior jobs in the police, but his early business ventures were mostly disastrous and as he approached the age of 40 in the late 1980s he was mired in debt. Then his luck changed: he snared several lucrative state telecommunications concessions between 1998 and 1991, and made the most of the wild bubble years before 1997 to build a multi-billion-dollar fortune. His parliamentary career followed a similar trajectory: an initial foray into politics in the mid-1990s was a debacle but by the end of the decade he was ready to try again, and achieved stunning success.

Thaksin set up a new political vehicle – Thai Rak Thai, or 'Thais Love Thais' – and adopted a remarkably eclectic approach towards party personnel and policies. He made the effort to build a policy platform that appealed to several crucial political support bases: the traditional royalist Chinese Thai business elite, who regarded him as a natural ally; small business owners and employees resentful of IMF-imposed austerity measures; and the rural poor. He used modern marketing methods supported by a hefty advertising budget to establish awareness of the Thai Rak Thai brand, message and policy platform. Other parties didn't even *have* a brand, message or policy platform. Thaksin stormed to victory in the January 2001 general election, coming just two seats short of an overall majority, the best result any party had achieved in Thai history.

After taking office, Thaksin's administration promptly and efficiently began implementing his policy pledges. For voters weary of decades of broken political promises, this was another welcome sign of change. His approval ratings soared. Pasuk and Baker note how radical all this was:

> In February 2001, Thaksin Shinawatra, one of Thailand's richest businessmen, became prime minister and appointed a Cabinet studded with other leading business figures. This was new. Although businessmen had dominated Thailand's parliament as electoral politics developed over the previous two decades, big business figures had remained slightly aloof. Thaksin had won the election on a platform of measures appealing directly to the rural mass. This too was new. Previous elections had been won by local influence. Party platforms had not been taken seriously… Thaksin's party had won just short of an absolute majority. In no previous election since 1979 had any party reached one third. Over the coming year, Thaksin implemented all the major elements of his electoral platform. This was very new indeed. (Pasuk and Baker, 2009b)

Thaksin was the first Thai leader in decades to take electoral politics seriously and actively seek a sustainable mandate from voters. But he also sought to cultivate approval from the palace. During the 1990s, he donated heavily to Sirikit and the profligate and perennially cash-strapped Vajiralongkorn (Handley, 2006a). In a leaked cable, Boyce noted that 'the King will not be around forever, and Thaksin long ago invested in Crown Prince futures' (05BANGKOK2219).

During the first year of his premiership, Thaksin had the support of most of the establishment, particularly Sirikit's circle. But the king loathed him. Bhumibol had always been suspicious of civilian politicians and was livid about Thaksin's funding of the crown prince, which sabotaged the king's efforts to bring his son to heel by restricting his financial allowance. In his birthday speech in December 2001 he mocked the prime minister in a monologue with derision, to Thaksin's obvious discomfort. In early 2002, the *Far Eastern Economic Review* published a report on Bhumibol's annoyance at Thaksin's 'attempts to meddle in royal family affairs' and his 'business links' with Vajiralongkorn, based on information leaked by elite sources (*Far Eastern Economic Review*, 2002). Thaksin's government reacted furiously, threatening to expel the magazine's correspondents in Bangkok, which gave further credence to the report.

Meanwhile, Thaksin began relentlessly sabotaging the checks and balances put in place by the 1997 constitution and rendering them toothless. This was a direct challenge to Prem Tinsulanonda, who wielded immense influence behind the scenes as the leading figure in the network monarchy. 'Thaksin set about systematically to dismantle the political networks loyal to Prem in a wide range of sectors, aiming to replace them with his own supporters, associates and relatives', explains McCargo. 'Thaksin was seeking to subvert network monarchy, and to replace it with ... a network based on insider dealing and structural corruption.' Prem had expected the prime minister to follow the unwritten code of the elite and do as he was told. But 'Thaksin had no intention of following these gentlemanly rules of the game' and 'proceeded to freeze Prem out of key decisions, demonstrating his determination to create a new supernetwork, centred entirely on himself' (McCargo, 2005).

By 2005, most elite Thais had turned against Thaksin. The ethnic Chinese tycoons feared he would use his political dominance to assert his own economic interests at their expense. The liberal wing of the establishment was appalled at his disregard for checks and balances, freedom of speech and the rule of law. Prem and his conservative allies were infuriated by Thaksin's efforts to neutralize their extra-constitutional influence and build his own power network.

In the first half of 2005, two bombshells transformed the elite's disquiet into full-blown panic. In February, Thai Rak Thai won an extraordinary general election landslide, securing 375 of parliament's 500 seats. Thaksin became the first prime minister ever re-elected for a second consecutive term, and the first to win an overall parliamentary majority at the polls. After decades of fragmented parliaments and fractious coalition governments, Thailand was moving towards a two-party system with the Democrat Party the only viable opposition. In the aftermath of their crushing defeat, the Democrats selected a seemingly more electable leader, Abhisit Vejjajiva, but there seemed to be no prospect of them mounting an effective challenge to Thaksin for years – the party was elitist, hidebound and devoid of new ideas. The likelihood of Thaksin dominating parliament for decades on the basis of populist policies aimed at the poor was profoundly worrying to the traditional establishment.

In April, Vajiralongkorn's third wife Srirasmi Akharapongpreecha gave birth to a son. The crown prince had a legitimate male heir once again. The ruling class had long been confident that when the time came they would be able to keep Vajiralongkorn off the throne and engineer the accession of a more acceptable monarch, as had routinely happened throughout Thai history. But by 2005 their optimism was evaporating. The birth of a son changed the calculus dramatically – the elite's preferred candidate for monarch, Sirindhorn, had never married and had no children. Suddenly the crown prince was in a much stronger position.

Moreover, Thaksin's apparent alliance with the prince made it less implausible that Vajiralongkorn could become king. The prime minister's unprecedented approval ratings and electoral mandate could compensate for the crown prince's unpopularity. Together, they could make a formidable team, perhaps able to dominate Thailand for decades to come.

Fear of a looming era of political and financial dominance by Thaksin and Vajiralongkorn that would end the supremacy of the traditional establishment was what created the extraordinary climate of apocalyptic dread among the elite from 2005 onwards. A coalition assembled to combat Thaksin. It included almost the entire establishment, the military top brass, the Democrat Party, the bureaucracy and judiciary, and moralistic middle-class Bangkok royalists. What united them was not simply dislike of Thaksin, it was fear of Vajiralongkorn. From the start, the royal succession was central to their motivations.

Establishment statesmen became increasingly strident in their attacks on Thaksin. Meanwhile, a middle-class mass movement was rallied by a former supporter of the prime minister, media tycoon Sondhi Limthongkul. The king and queen were not party to the scheming to sabotage the succession; Sirikit still staunchly supported her son's claim to the throne, and, despite his dismay at Vajiralongkorn's behaviour, Bhumibol's conservatism meant he saw no real alternative either. The uncomfortable secret of the forces allied against Thaksin was that they wanted to defy the wishes of the king and sabotage the succession of the designated heir to the throne. To disguise this, they adopted shrill ultra-royalist rhetoric. Sondhi used a weekly television show to relentlessly denounce government corruption, and when Thaksin forced it off the air began holding regular rallies and broadcasting them via his satellite and cable channels and over the Internet. He routinely wore a yellow T-shirt with the slogan: 'I will fight for the king'. His supporters began to festoon themselves in the king's colour too. The 'Yellow Shirt' movement was born. Because of the taboos forbidding public discussion of the succession or criticism of the prince – and the grave risks that breaking them would entail – the movement's leaders never made explicit their opposition to Vajiralongkorn. But the clues were everywhere. Channelling decades of fear and loathing for the prince, establishment grandees and Yellow Shirt leaders made hysterical claims that Thaksin was a uniquely evil and corrupt figure who was leading the country into a dark age. In contrast to the millenarian uprisings of the past, in which the poor were motivated by the belief that a holy leader could build a fairer society, this was an uprising of Thailand's wealthy who feared that a malignant monarch would destroy their privileges.

The campaign to topple Thaksin faced the obvious problem that he was the most popular prime minister in Thai history. In terms of supporters, Thaksin overwhelmingly had the numbers on his side. But this was another theatrical legitimacy contest rather than a struggle that would be won or lost by brute strength. By mobilizing protesters week after week in Bangkok, Thaksin's opponents sought to create the impression that he had lost legitimacy, even though the Yellow Shirts clearly did not represent the majority opinion. They hoped to provoke Thaksin into overreacting and launching a crackdown, ideally involving excessive use of force that caused casualties among the protesters, as in 1973 and 1992. This would provide a pretext for the palace or military to step in. As Boyce observed, 'The anti-Thaksin forces are reduced to hoping for help from two extremes – the street, and the palace.

There is some irony here: the democratic opposition and civil society are pinning their short term hope on rather undemocratic solutions' (05BANGKOK7197). In a typically indiscreet interview in 2007, Sondhi said his elite backers had encouraged him to seek violent confrontation during the Yellow Shirt rallies: 'The request for military intervention or for the king to come out has always had one prerequisite: there must be bloodshed... I always had people calling me: "Khun Sondhi, could you move things a little bit forward, have a little confrontation, let us see a little blood?"' (Crispin, 2007).

Under pressure from mounting street protests, Thaksin made a series of poor decisions. In January 2006 he announced the sale of his Shin Corp conglomerate to Singapore sovereign wealth fund Temasek for $1.8 billion in the largest corporate deal in Thai history. Thaksin believed this would put a stop to accusations of policy corruption, but his opponents used the fact he had paid no tax on the sale to stir up middle-class outrage. On 4 February, up to 100,000 Yellow Shirt protesters staged a huge anti-government rally. On the morning of the protest, Thaksin made a rash statement in his weekly radio address, declaring: 'It would only take one person to remove me from office: ... His Majesty the King. If he whispered in my ear "Thaksin, it's time to go", I would certainly prostrate myself at his feet and resign.' His enemies accused him of insulting the palace. The Yellow Shirt movement gained renewed strength from these missteps, and another high-profile figurehead joined – Chamlong Srimuang, who had led the May 1992 protests. The Yellow Shirts also adopted a formal name – the People's Alliance for Democracy (PAD).

On 24 February, just a year after winning the most resounding mandate in Thai history, Thaksin called a snap election, believing another crushing victory at the polls would restore his legitimacy and silence his critics. The Democrat Party refused to take part. There were no valid arguments that boycotting would benefit Thailand's people, but the Democrats knew they would lose and so sought to engineer a constitutional crisis instead. Prem, the head of the privy council, told Boyce: 'The people want another prime minister' (06BANGKOK1767). But, in fact, Thailand's people had shown in the 2005 election that most of them wanted Thaksin. It was the old elite who wanted him gone.

The snap election on 2 April demonstrated Thailand's deepening polarization. Thai Rak Thai received about 16 million votes, 53 per cent of all votes cast. Nearly 10 million people chose the 'abstain' option on the ballot – essentially a vote against Thaksin – and there were nearly 4 million invalid votes. On 4 April, Thaksin travelled to Hua Hin for an audience with the king. A few hours later, after returning to Bangkok, he made a televised address to the nation. Ashen faced, he announced that he would not be prime minister in the next parliament. After his speech, Thaksin and his wife wept.

Comments from multiple sources, including Thaksin himself, in leaked US cables suggest he had decided before his audience with the king that he would make a tactical retreat and relinquish the premiership for a while. He intended to install a proxy and govern from behind the scenes. When he told the king he would not take the position of prime minister in the next government, Bhumibol merely nodded (06BANGKOK2149, 06BANGKOK2990, 06BANGKOK3180). A few hours later, Thaksin received a phone call from the king's principal private secretary Arsa Sarasin telling him that stepping down as prime minister was not enough and he needed to abandon politics entirely. This was what prompted his tearful speech to the country. Thaksin initially assumed Arsa had been conveying the king's orders, but later concluded that members of the palace network had manipulated the situation without Bhumibol's explicit authorization. At a meeting with a former White House official, a furious Thaksin 'spun an elaborate tale of palace intrigue, accusing privy councilors ... of conspiring against him':

> He claimed that courtiers in the palace are manipulating the infirm and isolated King. Thaksin repeated his theory that the King sees Thaksin as rival for the loyalty of the people in the countryside. Thaksin denied trying to rival the King, saying that he was a just a 'simple peasant' who wanted to be among the people and eat in noodle shops. He described the King, with barely-concealed disdain, as 'provincial', unaware of the changes that had taken place in the world ('never been on a Boeing 747'), and accused him of 'thinking he owns the country.' (06BANGKOK2990)

The political intrigues of March and April 2006 marked a decisive escalation of Thailand's elite conflict. This was the period when Thaksin belatedly realized the establishment wanted to crush his political influence, and when – after initial hesitation – he decided to fight back. The shadow boxing was over. An open battle for supremacy had begun.

On 25 April 2006, Bhumibol made his most overt and damaging intervention in years, in two televised speeches to judges. Striving to maintain the pretence of constitutional rule, Bhumibol dismissed calls for royal intervention to solve the political crisis. 'Asking for a royally appointed prime minister is undemocratic', he said. 'It is, pardon me, a mess. It is irrational.' Instead, the king declared, the judiciary should fix the constitutional crisis. Making clear what solution he preferred, the king said the April snap election was 'not democratic', hinting that the judiciary should find a way to nullify it. 'Otherwise', he said, 'the country will collapse' (*The Nation*, 2006c). Bhumibol failed to grasp that openly telling the judiciary what to do was no better than direct intervention. Indeed, it was worse, because it involved the explicit politicization of institutions that were supposed to be impartial. Governance and the rule of law had always been weak in Thailand, and always favoured the elite; during his five years in office Thaksin had managed to co-opt many of the institutions that were supposed to act as checks and balances. By explicitly signalling that the judiciary and state agencies should find a way to thwart Thaksin's political ambitions, the king undermined any semblance of justice or fairness. Instead of waging their struggle within an accepted constitutional framework, both sides sought to win any way they could. The result, as Michael Connors observes, was a 'ravine-like political division over the rules that define the acceptable exercise of power' (Connors, 2011).

In May 2006, the Constitutional Court ruled the election invalid, as Bhumibol had instructed. The decision enabled Thaksin to escape his promise to step down: he announced he would stay on as 'caretaker' prime minister until new elections were held. Meanwhile, senior privy councillors, judges and retired generals began actively plotting a coup. Details of one dinner party where the plan was discussed were leaked three years later by one of those present (Suthichai, 2009). The host of the dinner party, a minor royal called Piya Malakul, also began trying to undermine Sirikit's support for Thaksin. He told US diplomats he had 'spent three days with the Queen' convincing her that Thaksin was funding anti-monarchy websites and turning her against the prime minister (06BANGKOK3916).

Both sides were obliged to suspend overt hostilities during the Diamond Jubilee celebrations for Bhumibol in June, and then recommenced their open warfare immediately afterwards. At the end of the month, in a speech to bureaucrats and military officers, Thaksin explicitly stated that somebody abusing extra-constitutional royal power was actively plotting to overthrow him. It was a clear reference to Prem, and the accusation was undoubtedly true. Particularly because of its accuracy, it enraged the establishment. On 14 July, the 85-year-old Prem donned his full cavalry uniform for an extraordinary speech to military cadets, declaring: 'In horse racing, horse owners hire jockeys to ride the horses. The jockeys do not own the horses. They just ride them. A government is like a jockey. It supervises soldiers, but the real owners are the country and the King' (Suthichai, 2006). Three days later, the army announced an unexpected reshuffle that moved officers supportive of Thaksin – in particular his former classmates from cadet school – out of key positions in Bangkok and the north-east. The military was preparing for its putsch.

ELEVEN

'Coupmakers' haunted dreams'
Escalation and enlightenment

In the evening of 19 September 2006, tanks from outside the capital, commanded by generals loyal to Prem, trundled into the centre of Bangkok, some getting snarled in the rush-hour traffic. They parked outside government buildings and television stations. There was no fighting or bloodshed – as usual, the coup was a theatrical performance by the military to provide the elite with a cover story for suspending democracy. Bhumibol could have refused to endorse it and ordered the army back to the barracks. The royalist generals nominally leading the putsch would have been obliged to obey him. It had been fifteen years since the last coup and most Thais had believed the days of regular military takeovers were over. But the king had no objection to the military overthrowing the prime minister he despised. The junta named itself the 'Council for Democratic Reform under the Constitutional Monarchy', but later changed its English-language title to the 'Council for Democratic Reform' – the generals were eager to proclaim their royalist sympathies to Thais while trying to conceal from the international community that the king had willingly acquiesced in their coup. The US embassy noted that the junta was struggling with 'angst over how to portray the King's role' (06BANGKOK5929).

The 2006 coup was a catastrophic strategic miscalculation by the establishment, and Bhumibol's acquiescence was a disaster for the palace. Thaksin was the most popular prime minister Thailand ever had. His removal infuriated millions, particularly among the poor. The coup was the beginning of the end of mass reverence for the monarchy. Moreover, the establishment had assumed that Prem's coup was just the first stage of a plan he had agreed with the king to manage the succession. But it quickly became clear that Prem had not made any arrangements with Bhumibol to keep Vajiralongkorn off the throne. Thaksin also refused to meekly accept being turfed out of power. He fought back, and the elderly men who had seized control of the government were utterly befuddled about how to respond. US embassy contacts in north-east Thailand reported that 'local farmers could not accept that Thaksin has been ousted' (06BANGKOK6085). The coup solved none of the establishment's problems. It only made them worse. Writing under a pseudonym in *The Nation*, Pasuk and Baker commented that the elite were 'marooned on an island':

> On one side there is a sea of international opinion, appalled at how the beacon of democracy in Southeast Asia could have bombed itself back into the political stone age. On the other is the rural mass, probably unsurprised but massively resentful at this treatment of the first political leader they had embraced as their own. Why should they ever again listen to city slickers preaching to them about democracy? ...
> Reconciliation does not come out of the barrel of a gun. Unity cannot descend from above. The coup makers themselves are divided; the armed forces are divided; and the country is now divided worse than before. Moreover, things are likely to get worse. ('Chang Noi', 2006)

The junta installed one of Prem's allies, Surayud Chulanont, as prime minister. He chose a cabinet of twenty-six mostly elderly bureaucrats, academics, judges and retired military officers. It was quickly dubbed the 'cabinet of old men' and proved itself to be among the most abject and incompetent administrations in Thailand's history. As the cabinet floundered, the junta became increasingly uneasy and paranoid. The generals revived the anti-communist military organization ISOC to root out support for Thaksin. Trapped in an outdated Cold War mindset, the military leadership had no real understanding of modern Thailand and thought old solutions could fix new challenges. They scrambled to find evidence of Thaksin's corruption that could be used against him, and after months in office had come up with nothing.

On New Year's Eve, several bombs exploded around Bangkok. Three people were killed and several wounded. The government quickly blamed Thaksin but provided no evidence, and the investigation went nowhere. In a cable entitled 'Coupmaker's Haunted Dreams', Boyce reported comments from a political insider that junta leaders were 'not sleeping well at night'. 'Before the new year's bombing, many of the coup's early supporters were disillusioned and impatient; since the bombing, many seem angry and afraid', Boyce noted (07BANGKOK311). In another cable in February 2007 he discussed the establishment's infighting and incompetence:

> The ruling class of the country, in short, is acting like a room full of school kids with a substitute teacher... There may be one good result from all this: last year, we heard many education contacts in Bangkok complain that western-style democracy might not be suited to Thailand. They yearned for governance by 'good men', educated and professional, who did not have to win office through the corrupting procedure of partisan elections. Well, that's what they have now, and it clearly isn't working out so well. (07BANGKOK712)

Worsening the anxiety of the elite was the realization that Bhumibol could die at any time, radically altering the political landscape. They feared Thaksin and the crown prince would seek vengeance for the establishment's efforts to undermine them. A worried senior general told Boyce in April 2007 that he 'could not rule out the deposed PM returning and wreaking havoc on the country – and possibly acting vengefully' (07BANGKOK2280).

In another clumsy use of the judiciary to weaken Thaksin, Thai Rak Thai was dissolved in May and all 111 members of the party executive banned from holding political office for five years over alleged electoral offences in 2006. The ruling was particularly indefensible because it involved the retroactive application of a penalty that had been introduced after the coup. In June 2007 the junta struck another blow at Thaksin, seizing $1.7 billion of his wealth. In response, Thaksin began organizing mass demonstrations in Bangkok and around the country, under the banner of the United Front for Democracy against Dictatorship (UDD), which would later become known as the Red Shirt movement. He was emulating the tactics of the Yellow Shirts, and challenging the incumbent government via street politics. Thaksin also bought British football club Manchester City, a move McCargo describes as 'a brilliant public relations exercise, allowing him to remain constantly in the popular eye through Thailand's relentless television coverage of the English national game – in which he remained sublimely uninterested' (McCargo, 2009). The scale of the junta's defeat in their publicity battle became humiliatingly apparent when Thaksin bankrolled a Thai-themed party for 8,000 fans in the heart of Manchester and triumphantly strode onto the stage wearing a blue-and-white City scarf to join the singing of team anthem 'Blue Moon'.

Increasingly panicked, leading members of the establishment in Prem's circle launched a campaign to try to smear the crown prince and ruin his chances of becoming king. In mid-2007, a video was leaked showing Srirasmi's birthday party in Nonthaburi Palace in 2001, at which she had been virtually naked in the presence of numerous courtiers as the crown prince looked on, contentedly puffing on his pipe. A confidential US cable noted that 'some in palace circles are working actively to undercut whatever support exists for the Royal Consort, and we assume that this undercurrent also has implications for the Crown Prince' (07BANGKOK5718).

As the elite secretively plotted over the royal succession, popular faith in the monarchy was collapsing. On 19 August, the government held a referendum on a new draft constitution to replace the 1997 charter. Voting against it was futile as this would allow the government to impose any constitution it wanted from Thailand's history, according to the rules the elite had written to ensure an outcome that suited them. A huge military-backed propaganda campaign told Thais that voting to reject the charter was tantamount to voting against Bhumibol, using the slogan 'Love the King. Care about the King. Vote in the referendum. Accept the 2007 draft charter'. Copies of the draft constitution were distributed with a yellow cover – the king's colour. The revived ISOC internal security agency coordinated the campaign, using 50,000 troops to go door-to-door across the country telling people to vote 'Yes'. In Bangkok, police raided the office of a well-known democracy activist and confiscated campaign material opposing the constitution, including posters with the slogan 'It's not illegal to vote against the draft constitution'. Bangkok taxi drivers – who tended to be staunch Thaksin supporters – were warned not to display bumper stickers with the message 'I accept passengers; I don't accept the new constitution'. In spite of all this, more than 42 per cent of those who cast their ballots voted 'No'. This was a remarkable result. Given the fact that an opinion poll would be unthinkable, it is difficult to estimate what percentage of Thais genuinely revere the monarchy. The 2007 referendum is probably the best gauge, and suggests that the number of royalists is far lower than the establishment likes to claim.

In October 2007, Bhumibol suffered a stroke and was hospitalized for nearly a month. The king's deputy principal private secretary, Tej Bunnag, told Boyce that Bhumibol had clearly signalled that the crown prince was his chosen heir. As a leaked cable recounted:

> Tej explained that the King had very much wanted to participate in the November 5 royal barge procession. Given his medical condition, Palace figures prepared five alternatives for his consideration. When they presented these, however, the King quickly dismissed them. According to Tej, the King said, 'I don't need these; the Crown Prince is my representative.' ... Tej said Palace insiders interpreted the King's blunt decision as the clearest indication yet of his determination to have the Crown Prince retain his current status as the King's designated successor. (07BANGKOK5738)

In the general election in December, the Thaksin-controlled People's Power Party won 233 seats, not far short of an absolute majority. The Democrat Party won just 165. 'The 2007 election provided a useful indicator of the limits of Palace influence', observed incoming US ambassador Eric John:

> Plausible rumors in the period leading up to the election claimed that Queen Sirikit sought actively to block the return to power of pro-Thaksin forces. We may attribute the failure of such efforts to divisions within the royal family, or to the lack of mechanisms

to effectively convey Palace views to the public while maintaining
plausible claims that the Chakri dynasty plays an appropriately
apolitical role. (08BANGKOK1293)

'The coup is dead', declared Samak Sundaravej, the 72-year-old
ultra-royalist whom Thaksin selected as his proxy prime minister
(*The Nation,* 2007). On 28 February 2008, Thaksin returned from
exile, prostrating himself on the ground outside Suvarnabhumi
Airport as thousands of supporters cheered and wept. These were
crushing blows to the old establishment. Thaksin was back in
control of parliament. Vajiralongkorn still seemed set to become
Rama X. The coup had achieved nothing:

> After two years of uncertainty, including massive demonstrations,
> an annulled election, a caretaker government, a military coup, a
> junta, an interim government and a new constitution, we are pretty
> much back to where we were in 2005. There has been no resolution
> of the issues that provoked the crisis in the first place. The rule
> of law and accountability for elected officials have not been
> strengthened, the corrupting role of money in the political process
> has not been reduced, the relationship between politicians and the
> royal institutions, including the Privy council, has not be clarified.
> After a strategic pause, the same conflicts that led to the political
> crisis are likely to re-emerge. (08BANGKOK198)

But within a few months, the despondency and fear that had
gripped the elite in 2007 evaporated, replaced by a giddy mood of
exuberant combativeness. The reason was Sirikit. The queen had
become increasingly extremist following her split with Bhumibol
in the mid-1980s. Sirikit's belief that she was a reincarnation
of Suriyothai prompted her to enlist a royalist prince in the
late 1990s to produce *The Legend of Suriyothai*, a costly epic
movie. She had always been Vajiralongkorn's staunchest supporter; however, egged on by her ladies-in-waiting, who indulged
her fantasies of being a reborn warrior queen and hated the

crown prince, by April 2008 she had pledged her full support to Sondhi's PAD and decided to freeze her son out of the royal succession, planning to reign as regent when Bhumibol died, on behalf of Vajiralongkorn's young son Dipangkorn. It was a questionable plan, not least because Sirikit was approaching the age of 76 and her health was not much better than her husband's. Also, Bhumibol was implacably against it. He had been estranged from his wife for two decades. Although he had grave misgivings about his son, he was even more appalled by the idea of Sirikit effectively succeeding him. Had royalist veneration of Bhumibol been genuine, his opposition to their succession machinations would have put an end to the scheming. But for the elite, self-preservation was far more important than principle. Bhumibol's objections were ignored.

To have any hope of success, the plan required three institutions to be on board. First, the privy council was crucial - if Bhumibol died without removing Vajiralongkkorn's status as heir, the privy council could still propose an alternative candidate by invoking Article 10 of the 1924 Palace Law on Succession, which states:

> The Heir who is to succeed to the Throne should be fully respected by the people and the people should be able to rely on him happily. If he is considered by the majority of the people as objectionable, he should be out of the line to the Throne.

Second, the army leadership had to agree. If the military opposed efforts to meddle with the royal succession they would crush the plot. Third, under Thailand's constitution, parliament has to formally ratify the privy council's decision and proclaim the new monarch. There would be no time to circumvent this by staging a coup and appointing a new parliament because another crucial element of the plan was that it would have to be executed with decisive speed.

The privy council was fully on board – Prem was a prime mover in the plan to sabotage the succession, and his elderly allies all loathed Vajiralongkorn. The army leadership also supported blocking the prince. The problem was parliament. Ever since the start of the twenty-first century, Thaksin had won control of parliament every time an election was held, even when the odds were heavily stacked against him. Given the fecklessness of the Democrat Party, there was no prospect of this changing. Some way had to be found to prise parliament from Thaksin's grip. Apparently oblivious of the damage it would do to the reputation of the monarchy, and unconcerned that they had failed to accomplish anything after grabbing control of parliament in the disastrous coup of September 2006, the establishment decided to try to topple the elected government and seize control of the legislature all over again. During 2008 Thailand experienced an extraordinary phenomenon: an insurgency by the elite and Bangkok middle class against their own elected government, with direct support from the queen. The Yellow Shirt movement became increasingly extremist and aggressive. 'Thailand was firmly in the grip of "late reign" national anxiety, which formed the basic explanation for the otherwise illegible performances and processions of the PAD', observes McCargo:

> As time went on, the PAD became captives of their own rhetoric, unable to converse with others, let alone back down or make compromises. Rather than seek to build broad support for their ideas, core leaders made vitriolic speeches – for which Sondhi set the tone – in which they denounced anyone critical of, or unsympathetic to, their actions. Such megaphone posturing served to alienate potential supporters, and to strengthen the

PAD's dangerous sense of themselves as an in-group of truth-tellers and savants, whose nationalist loyalties were not properly appreciated or understood. This self-presentation had distinctly cultic overtones, and Sondhi's own language became increasingly demagogic. (McCargo, 2009)

On 25 May, the Yellow Shirts attempted to march on parliament and Government House. After being stopped at the nearby Makkawan Bridge, they set up a permanent protest site there. It was the beginning of 193 days of increasingly disruptive protest intended to sabotage the government's ability to govern. Sondhi's anti-democratic beliefs were made clear when he began proposing that 70 per cent of parliament should be appointed by the establishment and only 30 per cent elected. The proposal was motivated by a determination to put parliament forever beyond Thaksin's control and ensure Vajiralongkorn could be prevented from becoming king.

Meanwhile, the courts continued delivering judgments damaging to the Thaksin camp. On 8 July, the Supreme Court upheld electoral fraud charges against a senior ally of Thaksin. The decision meant that the PPP could face dissolution according to the rules of the 2007 constitution. The judiciary also stepped up its efforts to convict Thaksin and his wife Pojaman on corruption charges over a 2003 deal. During August, Thaksin and Pojaman travelled to China for the Beijing Olympics. Instead of returning to Thailand afterwards, they flew to London. Thaksin faxed a handwritten statement to the Thai media declaring he would not return to face legal proceedings he denounced as unfair. He was officially on the run.

Behind the scenes, the establishment was plotting to overthrow the government and engineer the appointment of a pliant prime minister. Royalist grandee Anand Panyarachun was touted as the most likely candidate, and admitted to US diplomats he was in contact with the plotters, adding: 'I cannot rule out regime change, but it would not be a traditional coup d'etat' (08BANGKOK2610). The establishment and Yellow Shirt movement faced the same problem as in 2005/6 – most Thais didn't support them. So the anti-Thaksin bloc sought to undermine the government's legitimacy however it could, while also trying to provoke a violent overreaction that would provide a pretext for a coup. Democrat Party MP Kraisak Choonhavan told US diplomats that 'the PAD hoped to provoke clashes with the police, leading to enough violence and government overreaction to spark military intervention/ another coup' (08BANGKOK2546).

On 26 August, the PAD stormed and occupied Government House during a day of coordinated provocations. On 29 August they raised the stakes again, forcing the shutdown of several provincial airports including Phuket, Krabi and Hat Yai, and blocking key railway services. Thousands of Thais and foreign tourists were stranded. In September, prime minister Samak was toppled by a Constitutional Court ruling that the prime minister had violated conflict-of-interest rules by continuing to appear on a television cookery programme, even though he received only nominal payments. It was an obviously partisan decision that made it clearer than ever that the judiciary was a tool of the elite to thwart the democratic will of the majority. Thaksin's brother-in-law Somchai Wongsawat was nominated as the next prime minister.

Somchai was scheduled to deliver his policy statement to parliament on 7 October. The Yellow Shirts again sought a confrontation that would legitimize a coup. Royalist tycoon Chutinant Bhirombhakdi reported that a senior Yellow Shirt leader admitted the PAD was hoping that at least two dozen of its own supporters would be killed, according to a leaked US cable:

> Chutinant believed PAD continued to aim for a violent clash that would spark a coup. He asserted that he had dined on October 6 with a leading PAD figure ... who explained that PAD would provoke violence during its October 7 protest at the parliament. The unnamed PAD figure predicted (wrongly) that the Army would intervene against the government by the evening of October 7. Chutinant asserted to us that PAD remained intent on a conflict that would generate at least two dozen deaths and make military intervention appear necessary and justified. (08BANGKOK3317)

On the night of 6 October, the Yellow Shirts marched to parliament, erecting barricades with razor wire and booby traps. PAD guards with slingshots, metal bars, golf clubs and cudgels patrolled the perimeter. At dawn on 7 October, the battle began. Police ordered the protesters to end their blockade and, when they refused to move, fired tear-gas canisters. Yellow Shirts threw ping-pong bombs and firecrackers. There were some unusually power-ful explosions. Dozens were badly wounded, including several people who lost limbs. Protesters claimed tear-gas canisters had caused the injuries, while the police insisted the Yellow Shirts had detonated pipe bombs. Battles raged throughout the day. Yellow Shirts tried to ram several vehicles, including a lorry, into police lines. One policeman was deliberately run over by a Yellow Shirt in a pickup truck, which then reversed back over him.

During the afternoon, an explosion destroyed a stationary Cherokee jeep some distance from the fighting, killing Methee Chartmontri, a former police lieutenant colonel who was a senior PAD militiaman and brother-in-law of a Yellow Shirt leader. Methee's body was blown apart – one leg was still inside the vehicle, most of his corpse was blasted out of the wrecked jeep, and his hands were never found. The second fatality was Ang-khana Radappanyawut a 28-year-old business administration graduate from Bangkok's Assumption University and the eldest of three sisters. She had joined the protests that day with her family, all supporters of the Yellow Shirts. Angkhana died near the corner of Royal Plaza, in the thick of the battle, the left side of her chest torn open by a blast that lacerated her heart, stomach, spleen, left kidney and liver, and broke her left arm and all her ribs on the left side.

Once the fighting was over, establishment statesmen and anti-Thaksin newspapers sought to sensationalize the riot and smear the police and government. 'Bloodbath in Bangkok' was the front-page headline in *The Nation* (2008a). Porntip Rojana-sunan, a forensic pathologist and media celebrity, declared that her investigations showed the deaths and injuries had been caused by improper police use of tear gas. The establishment narrative of 'Black Tuesday' was a dictatorial government brutally suppressing peaceful protesters. Army commander Anupong Paochinda called on the prime minister to resign, declaring: 'No one can stay in a pool of blood' (*The Nation*, 2008b).

But the events of 7 October were a lethal pantomime deliber-ately enacted by anti-government forces to create conditions they hoped would induce military intervention. The protesters, not the police, had been the aggressors, as the US embassy noted: 'For most of the day, it was the PAD attacking police forma-tions, not the other way around. The police reported that PAD demonstrators utilized pistols, knives, and metal pipes during the clashes and also had gasoline-filled pingpong balls, essentially mini-Molotov cocktails' (08BANGKOK3042). Methee Chartmontri was killed by explosives he was transporting, which detonated prematurely, probably while he was holding them – the reason for his missing hands. Porntip's investigations were a sham: she based her findings on the use of the GT200, a fake explosives detector which was simply an empty plastic box with a swivelling metal antenna attached, lacking any mechanical or electrical parts or even a power source. It had initially been sold online as a novelty dowsing rod for finding lost golf balls, but British conman Gary Bolton had repackaged the devices, which cost less than £5 to make, and sold them to foreign governments and militaries as an advanced explosives detection system for up to £10,000 apiece. Anybody with basic scientific knowledge would have realized there was no way the GT200 could work, but Porntip became an enthusiastic supporter of the device. When the scandal was revealed in 2010, she was exposed as a charlatan. The US embassy commented that her attempts to defend her use of the GT200 were 'inexplicable, the latest example of her increasingly erratic judgment in recent years' (10BANGKOK478). Nick Nostitz, one of the foreign journalists who covered the battle, described establishment efforts to manipulate the narrative as a 'game of smoke and mirrors' (Nostitz, 2008).

Six days after the battle, Queen Sirikit presided at Angkhana's cremation ceremony. Thousands of Yellow Shirts at the funeral chanted 'Long Live Her Majesty'. Afterwards, Angkhana's father wept as he told reporters: 'Her Majesty said my daughter was a good woman since she had helped the nation and preserved the monarchy' (Chalathip, 2008). Many Thais were shocked by Sirikit's overt support for an extremist anti-democratic movement which had deliberately provoked confrontation with the police in an effort to topple an elected government. As the US ambassador noted:

> Queen Sirikit ... made a bold political statement practically
> without precedent in presiding over the funeral of a PAD supporter
> from humble roots who died during the October 7 clash between
> PAD and the police. Even some figures close to the Queen have
> expressed their private unease at the overtly political act, since
> it seems to erode the concept, which the King has long sought
> to promote, of an apolitical monarchy. After the Queen's funeral
> appearance, there was a notable increase in public complaints
> about acts of lese majeste, with many seemingly targeting the
> Queen; PPP-affiliated politicians have expressed a combination
> of fear and loathing for the Queen in private conversations with
> us in recent months. Such politicization of the monarchy at this
> time appears to create extra uncertainty around the eventual royal
> succession, and it could well boomerang on royalists when the time
> comes to redefine the role of the monarchy after the King's passing.
> (08BANGKOK3289)

Supreme Court judges made Thaksin a convicted criminal
in October, sentencing him to two years in jail for corruption.
Bhumibol, meanwhile, was troubled by his wife's clumsy political
intervention and the antics of the Yellow Shirts – the king had
always hated chaos and unrest. The elderly monarch attempted to
intervene, sending a signal that he wanted the Yellow movement
to end its confrontational strategy. As usual, he did not say so
directly, but instructed three of the most trusted members of his
inner circle to convey the message. On 9 October, Sirindhorn
made a rare political comment at a news conference in the USA,
when asked whether the Yellow Shirts were acting in the monarchy's interests. 'I don't think so', she replied. 'They do things
for themselves.' Later in the month, Bhumibol again signalled his
opposition to continued Yellow Shirt disruption via comments by
two of his closest confidantes, Sumet Tantivejkul and Disathorn
Wathcharothai. Sumet told protesters to 'stop violence and secure
peace via dialogue'. Disathorn's statement was even more direct.

'If you love the king, go back home', he said. 'I carry the king's message' (09BANGKOK2167). But Yellow Shirt leader Sondhi didn't just ignore the king – he publicly denounced Bhumibol's messengers. It is inconceivable that he could have behaved with such swaggering insolence towards the monarch he claimed to revere unless he was very confident he had the backing of Sirikit and her allies in the establishment. Millions of Thais claimed to love the king so much they would die for him, and yet Bhumibol was unable even to persuade the protesters to stop.

On 25 November, thousands of Yellow Shirts occupied Bangkok's Suvarnabhumi International Airport. The military did nothing to end the blockade. 'The government was already a government in exile in its own country, functioning from Chiangmai in the north, where Prime Minister Somchai was based, protected by pro-government forces', Nostitz observes. 'It seemed that the security forces were not following government orders, the military were refusing to work with the police... Civil war seemed entirely possible, and likely to be coming within days' (Nostitz, 2009). With the airport blockade inflicting severe damage on Thailand's economy and reputation, on 2 December the Constitutional Court dissolved the PPP and banned the prime minister and other top party members from politics for alleged electoral infractions in 2007. Once again, the judiciary had played a key role in sabotaging Thai democracy.

The military put enormous pressure on Thaksin's allies to jump ship, wielding both carrot and stick – legislators were offered large financial inducements to switch allegiance, and the army told them there would be a coup unless they changed sides. Negotiations focused on a parliamentary faction controlled by the notoriously corrupt Newin Chidchob, previously an ally of

Thaksin who now agreed to betray him. In a phone call he told Thaksin: 'It's over, boss' (Tulsathit, 2008). On 15 December, parliament selected Abhisit as prime minister. The 'silent coup' of 2008 was complete. Parliament was back under the control of the old elite.

TWELVE

'Returning happiness to the people'
Denying democracy, sabotaging succession

Thailand regressed yet again to military dictatorship on 22 May 2014. Two days after imposing martial law with a televised declaration in the dead of night but insisting it was not seizing power, the army summoned the country's political leaders for peace talks and promptly arrested them when they arrived. To justify their coup, the military declared that political feuding had rendered Thailand ungovernable, and claimed they had only intervened as a last resort to save the kingdom from calamity and avert civil war.

Criticism of this absurd narrative was outlawed. Outspoken journalists and academics were rounded up and intimidated, held in military detention for days, and warned upon their release to keep quiet or face jail. Several chose to flee the country rather than turn themselves in. Independent television and radio stations were shut down, and the junta even briefly blocked access to Facebook. Thais were not only banned from complaining about the coup, they were ordered to be happy about it. Army chief Prayuth Chan-ocha, who had awarded himself the position of prime minister, began appearing on a weekly television show entitled *Returning Happiness to the People*. As the *Bangkok Post* reported:

> General Prayuth will be the key speaker and will talk about the work done by junta over the previous week and clarify issues in

the public interest, according to Colonel Sirichan Ngathong, the deputy National Council for Peace and Order spokeswoman.

General Prayuth will not answer questions from the public, and radio and television stations will be compelled to air the programme. (Thanida and Wassana, 2014)

The junta announced that Prayuth had even found the time to compose the lyrics to a new patriotic song, proclaiming the army's determination to heal Thailand:

Today the nation is facing menacing danger.
The flames are rising.
Let us be the ones who step in, before it is too late.
The land will be good soon.
Happiness will return to Thailand. (Khaosod English, 2014)

The coup was the culmination of years of slow strangulation of Thai democracy by the traditional elite. Making Abhisit prime minister in 2008 had failed to improve the establishment's position. His administration faced an insurmountable legitimacy deficit from the start. Until army-backed horse-trading propelled him to the premiership, Abhisit insisted new elections were the only solution to political deadlock. After he became prime minister he clung to power for almost thirty months without going to the polls to seek a democratic mandate. He professed distaste for the criminal actions of the PAD and the interventionism of the army, but allowed them to engineer his political ascent. He gave pedantic legalistic justifications for his right to rule, failing to acknowledge the outrage of Thais who had seen their democratically expressed wishes trampled. 'Their path to government has been anything but honourable', observed Andrew Walker, noting that it required 'the assistance of a military coup, two party dissolutions, a new constitution, an activist judiciary, royal backing, an ultra-nationalist crisis, six months of escalating street provocation, military insubordination, and an economically disastrous airport shutdown' (Walker, 2008).

Abhisit announced a policy of 'zero tolerance' for corruption upon taking office, but it was just posturing. He was dependent on the backing of Newin and his cronies, who were given control of three of the most lucrative ministries, in terms of potential for corruptly siphoning off funds – Transport and Communications, Commerce and Interior. The cabinet was full of incompetent ministers who owed their positions to political deal-making. Ranongrak Suwanchawee, wife of a faction leader who had been banned from politics, was appointed information and communications minister. She had been deputy finance minister – again on behalf of her husband – in the Samak administration. She had told her first news conference: 'I am trying to learn everything that is under my responsibility. As soon as I learned about my appointment, I did a search on the Internet to see what the Finance Ministry actually does.' The commerce minister was Pornthiva Nakasai, whose experience derived from managing a brothel. US ambassador John reported that at their first meeting Pornthiva 'had to read all of her points from a text' (08BANGKOK3774).

By early April 2009, Thaksin decided to seek to topple Abhisit's government through mass unrest. On 11 April, after several days of mounting protests, Red Shirts burst into the Royal Cliff Hotel in the sex resort of Pattaya, where world leaders were gathering for an international summit. Nine foreign heads of state – including the Japanese and Chinese prime ministers – fled from the roof of the hotel by helicopter. It was a humiliation for the government. In response, Abhisit launched a crackdown in Bangkok. Before dawn on 13 April, soldiers in full combat gear fired repeated volleys of automatic gunfire at Red Shirts and also used tear gas. The protesters fought back with firebombs, slingshots and rocks. But, unlike in 1973 and 1992, the military crackdown did not turn public opinion in Bangkok decisively in favour of the protesters. Although the army assault had been disproportionate, the Red Shirts lost considerable public support because of the violent actions of some of those among them.

The April 2009 crackdown fuelled the rage and bitterness felt by many Thais since the coup. But Abhisit and his government failed to understand the anger of ordinary people. They believed the Red Shirts were just pawns in a political game being played by Thaksin. There was some truth to this view – one of Thaksin's main lawyers was quoted as saying in a leaked US cable that during the confrontation Thaksin was attempting – and failing – to negotiate a deal via back-channel contacts with the elite (09BANGKOK974). But this was only part of the story. By ignoring the legitimate grievances of the Red Shirts, and a huge number of ordinary Thais who sympathized with them, the establishment failed to understand the seriousness of their legitimacy crisis. As Marc Askew says: 'The government blamed the red shirts for sowing the violence, and this condemnation overshadowed any interest in the reasons for ordinary red-shirt supporters' political rage' (Askew, 2010).

A few days later, the succession conflict erupted into the open, further tarnishing the image of the monarchy. The prime minister's preferred choice for police chief was opposed by Vajiralongkorn, who was trying to shore up his succession prospects by quietly taking control of key institutions. The crown prince persuaded Newin's faction and some Democrat Party members to back his candidate. Leading Democrats sought to enlist Sirikit's help to thwart the prince. Niphon Promphan, an adviser to the crown prince, who resigned from the Democrat Party over the issue, acknowledged to US diplomats that 'the perceived intervention was unhelpful both for the Crown Prince and the monarchy' (09BANGKOK2455). As his wife and son feuded, Bhumibol was unable even to stop the infighting in his own family, let alone restore national unity. He was a lonely, fading figurehead. 'We believe the King's purported influence actually far exceeds his actual ability to control events', stated a US cable:

> Now in the deep twilight of his long reign, the King remains deeply venerated by the vast majority of his subjects, and symbolically he remains the central pillar of Thai identity. Despite this adulation and symbolic importance, however, the evidence suggests his ability to influence current events in his Kingdom, on the rare occasions he attempts to do so, is on the wane. (09BANGKOK2167)

On 15 September 2009, Bhumibol went to Siriraj Hospital for a routine check-up. The following day, he was admitted to the hospital for further treatment. Official sources told diplomats that the king's condition was not serious, but as the days passed it became clear he had no intention of leaving hospital. He was to remain in Siriraj for almost four years. The king's behaviour remains a mystery, but several contacts of the US embassy speculated that he was suffering from severe depression. He may also have been trying to send a message to his subjects – for Thais who believe the monarch is a microcosm of his kingdom, a hospitalized king means a disordered and sick country. It is also possible he believed – rightly or wrongly – that he was at risk of being murdered. Paranoia had always characterized his reign, and by 2009 there were plausible reasons why the elite – and even his wife – might want him dead. Elections had to be held by 2011, and there was a strong possibility Thaksin would again win control of parliament.

If the elite wanted to keep Vajiralongkorn off the throne, it would be convenient for Bhumibol to die before the next election.

In late 2009 and early 2010, US ambassador Eric John visited some of Thailand's most influential elder statesmen: privy council chief Prem, who was 89 at the time; privy councillor Siddhi Savetsila, who had just turned 90; and former prime minister Anand Panyarachun, who was 78. All three lied to the US ambassador to conceal their active efforts to sabotage the succession, but all were scathing about Vajiralongkorn. Siddhi told the ambassador 'almost hopefully' that 'if the Crown Prince were to die, anything could happen' and perhaps Sirindhorn could be queen. He lamented the decline in support for the monarchy, 'noting that something as simple as excessive motorcade-related traffic jams caused by minor royals was an unnecessary but enduring irritant', and 'stories that the Crown Prince now ordered second story windows closed as his motorcade passed achieved nothing but additional popular resentment' (10BANGKOK192).

In early 2010, the judiciary geared up for another assault on Thaksin. The Supreme Court announced it would give its verdict on 26 February on whether more than $2 billion of Thaksin's frozen assets should be seized. Thaksin's supporters began preparing for what they billed as their 'final battle'. But there was increasing discord among the Red Shirt leadership over two issues. The first was dismay that Thaksin's narrow personal interests were being given too much importance when formulating strategy. As the US embassy remarked: 'the timing and nature of the upcoming protest is being dictated by Thaksin, with an eye on the expected February 26 Supreme Court decision on his frozen assets' (10BANGKOK380). Second, there were differences over whether violent resistance was acceptable. Rogue general Khattiya Sawasdipol had emerged as an influential member of Thaksin's circle, and announced that he was assembling a force of 1,000 paramilitary rangers to protect the Red Shirts. In comments to US diplomats, one of Thaksin's lawyers admitted Khattiya was 'a 'warlord' who might be put in play in the possible chaos of a messy transition scenario' (09BANGKOK3067). In early February, Red Shirt hardliners visited Thaksin in Dubai, announcing afterwards that a 'people's army' would be created. Other Red Shirt leaders distanced themselves from the plan, but as the US embassy commented: 'Thaksin's willingness to be photographed with those who embrace violence suggests a willingness to condone their methods as longs as it suits his purposes' (10BANGKOK340). Apparently trying to appear fair and hoping to lower tensions, the Supreme Court ruled that $1.4 billion of Thaksin's fortune should be seized but he could keep around $900 million he had made before becoming prime minister. But if the supposed compromise was intended to placate Thaksin, it failed. He launched another attempt to seize back power.

Thaksin's strategy was to stage the same deadly street theatre that has become traditional in political conflicts. A secret militia was assembled to mingle among the Red Shirts and use urban insurgency tactics to harass and attack soldiers. Khattitya was the public face of Thaksin's forces, but this was misdirection – the rogue general and his rangers were given a defensive role, to guard and fortify Red Shirt protest encampments. Meanwhile, a second militia of provocateurs, made up mostly of serving military personnel, was Thaksin's secret strike force. Making the situation even more combustible, the military was split. A rift between Red and Yellow ran right through the military. Most of the top brass were pro-Sirikit, but among more junior officers and rank-and-file soldiers there was significant sympathy for the Red Shirts. These troops were nicknamed 'watermelon' soldiers – green on the outside, red on the inside. Military disunity went beyond Red versus Yellow, however. In the twenty-first century the most senior positions had become dominated by a single clique, from the Queen's Guard. This caused bitterness in the traditionally dominant clique, the Bangkok-based 'Clan of Angels', or King's Guard. Their rivalry and mutual resentment mirrored the relationship between Sirikit and Bhumibol, and made Thailand's divisions even more perilous. In April and May 2010 the crisis entered a tragic new phase.

The Red Shirt uprising of 2010

In mid-March 2010, more than 100,000 Red Shirts converged on Bangkok from northern and north-eastern Thailand. Pro-establishment newspapers depicted them as a furious feral mob. 'Red rage rising' was the *Bangkok Post*'s front-page headline on 13 March. 'UDD rural hordes head for the capital' (*Bangkok Post*, 2010). During March there was a carnival atmosphere in the Red camp and at their rallies around the city. Thousands of Bangkok residents came out to cheer them on. But as March progressed, several government and military buildings were targeted by grenade attacks. On 28 and 29 March, negotiations were held between Abhisit and the Red leadership, broadcast live on Thai television. This was a welcome development, largely forgotten now in the light of the tragedy that followed. It brought a brief moment of much-needed transparency to Thai politics: instead of the elite seeking to decide the fate of the country via furtive back-room dealings, these negotiations could be watched by all. But Thaksin had no interest in polite negotiation that made everybody look good. After a few days, to the dismay of moderate Red leaders, Thaksin ordered an end to talks.

On 3 April, the Red Shirts occupied Ratchaprasong, turning the busy intersection into a sprawling urban village of makeshift tents housing food stalls, dormitories, shops and clinics, surrounded by barricades made from tyres and sharpened bamboo poles. Bangkok has long had a massive Lao population from Thailand's impoverished north-eastern Isaan region; they are the underclass who work in the suburban factories and sweatshops, drive the buses and tuktuks and motorbikes and taxicabs, clean corporate offices and affluent homes, and service the sexual appetite of customers of the massage parlours and sex bars of the capital's industrialized prostitution industry. Bangkok's more affluent residents used their services every day, but never paid them much attention, until suddenly they took control of 2 square miles of prime real estate in the middle of the modern city. For Bangkok's old establishment and increasingly prosperous and influential middle classes, it was an outrageous inversion of hierarchy, a violation of the fundamental rules that held their whole cosmos together. Ratchaprasong had become a zone of dangerous disorder, like the mass gathering of students in the grounds of Thammasat University in 1976, a very public challenge not only to the traditional ascendancy of the elite but also to the caste system in which the middle classes had carved out a privileged position. It provoked enormous anger among those who felt their elevated place in society was under threat.

On 10 April, the military launched an operation to clear the protesters out of their camps, firing tear gas and rubber bullets, and using a water cannon. The crowd fought back with iron bars, clubs and stones. Army helicopters dropped more tear gas, and were fired on by unknown shooters among the protesters. Around 4 p.m. soldiers fired live ammunition at protesters. But the operation was a failure, being unable to dislodge the protesters. A few hours after dark, violence erupted again, in the Dinso Road area.

The two military commanders on the ground, both closely linked to Sirikit's inner circle, were ambushed with grenades. The most senior officer was killed along with four other soldiers, while his deputy was gravely wounded. Soldiers panicked and began firing wildly, killing around twenty civilians, including Hiro Muramoto, a Japanese cameraman for Reuters. The assassins who provoked the violence have never been officially identified, but high-level sources say the grenade attacks were the work of disgruntled soldiers motivated by factional rivalry and working with an extremist Red Shirt faction operating independently of the mainstream movement and seeking to provoke a bloody confrontation.

After the violence of 10 April, the Red Shirts abandoned the battle-scarred Ratchadamnoen area, consolidating their hold on the Ratchaprasong intersection. Meanwhile, Thaksin's secret force of provocateurs set up camp in Lumphini Park, and launched harassing attacks on soldiers and police each night. As Human Rights Watch reported in an investigation,

> the attacks did not originate with Red Shirt Guards, but with a secretive armed element within the UDD whom protesters and media called the 'Black Shirts' or 'Men in Black' – though not all were dressed in black.
>
> Members of these armed groups were captured on photographs and film armed with various military weapons, including AK-47 and M16 assault rifles, as well as M79 grenade launchers, during their clashes with government security forces. (Human Rights Watch, 2011)

The militia used the tactics of urban insurgency, mounting hit-and-run attacks from within groups of peaceful protesters and then melting away. Most wore army-style uniforms or dressed like civilian protesters. They caused genuine fear and confusion among regular troops, most of whom never saw the 'Men in Black' even when under fire from them. On 22 April, M79 grenades, fired mortar-style from Lumphini by members of Thaksin's secret militia, hit the Sala Daeng Skytrain station and members of a pro-government faction who had rallied on Silom Road, killing one person and wounding scores. On 28 April, in chaotic clashes on a highway in northern Bangkok, soldiers fired live rounds at charging protesters. One soldier was killed, shot by accident by his own side.

In early May, in a televised address, Abhisit offered a 'peace roadmap', proposing elections in November and reforms to address social injustice among other concessions if the protesters ended their occupation. It was a remarkable victory for the protesters, and for common sense. As a result, it was unacceptable to hardliners on both sides. Neither Thaksin nor establishment extremists wanted a peaceful solution that required them to make concessions. The hawkish generals linked to the queen and Prem were disgusted by Abhisit's capitulation. After clarifying a few points of Abhisit's offer, the Red Shirt leadership tentatively accepted his terms, but following the direct intervention of Thaksin they began setting new conditions. This was intended to sabotage the truce by making demands that would isolate Abhisit and enrage the hawks on the Yellow side, and it worked. On 12 May, Abhisit withdrew his proposed concessions, saying the Reds had failed to grasp the opportunity of a peaceful resolution. Water and power supplies to the Red camp were shut off. Meanwhile, Thaksin's sabotage of the peace deal had split the Red leadership and left power in the hands of the more extreme elements. The moderates on both sides had been defeated by the hardliners.

On the evening of 13 May, Khattiya Sawasdipol was shot in the head by a sniper as he spoke to a *New York Times* journalist in the Red encampment. He died in hospital a few days later. From 14 May, violence spiralled as soldiers tightened their grip on areas around the Red encampment. Frequent gunfire and explosions rang out in several areas of downtown Bangkok and plumes of smoke from burning barricades darkened the sky. As Human Rights Watch reported:

Beginning on May 14, Thai security forces faced demonstrators who were better organized and resorted more quickly to violent tactics. Groups of mainly young men now openly attacked the army at the barricades, especially in Bon Kai and Din Daeng, using flaming tires, petrol bombs, slingshot-fired metal balls, and powerful homemade explosives and other weapons. Most of the young men who joined the fight at the barricades seemed to have little in common with the UDD protesters at the camp. On numerous occasions, Black Shirt militants appeared at the barricades to join the fight, firing assault weapons and M79 grenade launchers at soldiers.

Meanwhile, the military announced new rules of engagement that effectively enabled soldiers to shoot at anybody suspected of being a 'terrorist':

Human Rights Watch's investigations found that army snipers in buildings overlooking the protest sites, as well as soldiers on the defensive barricades on the ground, frequently fired on protesters who were either unarmed or posed no imminent threat of death or serious injury to the soldiers or others. Many of those whom soldiers targeted apparently included anyone who tried to enter the 'no-go' zone between the UDD barricades and army lines, or who threw rocks, petrol bombs, or burning tires towards the soldiers – from distances too great to be a serious threat to the soldiers' lines...

Video footage and eyewitness accounts show the army frequently fired into crowds of unarmed protesters, often wounding and killing several. (Human Rights Watch, 2011)

On 19 May, around dawn, troops breached the barricades of the Red encampment and scattered the protesters. Most of the Red Shirt leadership surrendered to police. In the chaotic hours that followed, dozens of buildings were targeted by arson attacks, and special forces soldiers firing from the Skytrain tracks killed six people inside the temple grounds of Wat Pathum Wanaram, which had been designated a safe haven for those fleeing the violence. The killings were so inflammatory that it appeared they were a deliberate provocation. Yet the soldiers involved insist they were under fire from armed provocateurs in front of the temple wall. They were exhausted, panicky and fighting a mostly unseen enemy. The most likely explanation is that soldiers fired indiscriminate bursts at actual or imagined 'Men in Black' in front of the temple, and their shots skewed high, as tends to happen when firing from an elevated position, going over the wall and into the compound. It was probably tragic incompetence.

The final death toll from two months of unrest was at least ninety-one, with more than 1,800 wounded.

When the violence was over, nobody had won. The legitimacy of the demands and grievances of the Red Shirt protesters was undermined by Thaksin's use of a secret militia to provoke confrontation. The government was hated by millions of Thais, who regarded Abhisit as a murderer. Popular reverence for the monarchy was falling apart.

In August 2011, Abhisit's administration was obliged to hold elections. The Democrat Party's election strategy showed how little its leaders understood Thailand's increasingly informed electorate. Thinking rural Thais were uneducated fools whose loyalty could be bought, and believing this had been the key to Thaksin's success, the Democrats had allowed Newin's Bhumjai Thai party to amass a massive war chest from control of key ministries to fund vote-buying across north and north-eastern Thailand. Bribery and attempted vote-buying had long been rife in Thai elections, with all parties guilty, and Thailand's people were smart enough to know that they could accept money from everybody who offered it and still vote for whomever they wanted. The military's ISOC state-within-a-state was enlisted to pressure Thais to vote for establishment parties, and army chief Prayuth

Chan-ocha exhorted citizens to 'elect good people ... good and polite ones who intend to work for the nation' (Walker, 2011). Ignoring the military, and proving once again that they were no fools, Thais overwhelmingly voted for the Pheu Thai party nominally led by one of Thaksin's younger sisters, Yingluck. Pheu Thai won 265 seats, an overall majority. The Democrats won just 159. The Bhumjai Thai party was decisively routed, winning only 34 seats – voters mostly took Newin's money and voted for Thaksin.

Thaksin was back on top. If Bhumibol died, Thaksin would be able to use parliament to block any attempt to sabotage the succession. Thaksin attempted to build bridges with the palace and military, concerned that another coup might be launched to overthrow his sister. The army's bloated annual budget was ring-fenced; the government avoided interference in military reshuffles. Draconian enforcement of the *lèse-majesté* law continued.

In December 2011, Bhumibol marked his 84th birthday – his seventh cycle. The mood in Thailand was bleak. Catastrophic floods had inundated large swathes of the country. Given the traditional association of the monarchy with mystical control over water, it was widely regarded as another illustration of Bhumibol's loss of authority. A 62-year-old grandfather, Ampon Tangnop-pakul, was sentenced to twenty years in prison in November for allegedly sending four text messages insulting the monarchy. The severity of the sentence shocked most Thais and overshadowed the king's birthday celebrations. Bhumibol was wheeled out of hospital and loaded into a Volkswagen van to be taken to the Grand Palace across the river. Thousands of Thais lined the route of the convoy, dressed in pink – believed to be an auspicious colour for the king's health – waving flags and clutching photographs. Wearing an ornate robe and seated on a golden throne, flanked by his wife and four children, Bhumibol gave a short speech from a balcony of the palace to the assembled ranks of politicians, generals and officials standing in the sweltering heat in the courtyard below. In a faltering voice, clutching the text with shaking hands, he intoned the same mantra he has been repeating for decades, calling on Thais to unite and do their duty. The sad spectacle symbolized the twilight of Thailand's traditional elite.

Thaksin scented victory. He believed his strategy of placating the military and the establishment would persuade them to agree to his return. In an interview with *Prachachat* newspaper in March 2012, his lawyer Noppadon Pattama said: 'They may see Thaksin or the Pheu Thai Party as a threat to the existence of the conservatives. But Thaksin has no policy to change the power structure of the country. So we want them to rest assured.' Asked how Thaksin was reassuring them, Noppadon replied: 'By showing that we are not a threat to the current status of their side. We are not doing anything which affects the main institution of the country. We do not show any overwhelming ambition to change the Defence Act, to interfere with the military reshuffle, or to amend Section 112 of the Criminal Code.' It was true: Thaksin had no intention of changing the power structure. He intended to install himself at the top of the existing hierarchy, as a prime minister who could dominate the country for decades, alongside Vajiralongkorn as king.

During 2012 and 2013 Thaksin's party made repeated attempts to find a way to secure an amnesty for him, demonstrating that its primary goal was to serve his narrow self-interest. The establishment fought these efforts using their control of supposedly impartial state institutions and by seeking to provoke street violence they hoped would lead to a mass uprising or a coup. A naked power struggle among two unprincipled elite factions was taking precedence over governance of the country. Thaksin's first plan to secure his homecoming involved 'reconciliation' proposals that included two highly controversial elements. The first, a broad amnesty for those involved in political violence in 2010, and even back to 2006, outraged the Red Shirts. The second, a voiding of all corruption charges brought against Thaksin by the junta that mounted the coup, outraged everybody else. Thaksin believed that offering his opponents an amnesty would persuade them to drop his criminal conviction in return. On 19 May 2012, thousands of Red Shirts rallied at Ratchaprasong to mark the crushing of their protest two years earlier. In comments via video link, which angered Red Shirts across the country, Thaksin thanked them for their help and said they were no longer needed: 'Today, we have reached the end of our path. It is like the people have rowed me in a boat to the bank. From now on it is about climbing a mountain. For this, I have to get into a car. The people do not need to carry the boat on their shoulders and send me up the mountain.'

Thaksin had failed to understand that the elite were determined to prevent him coming home. The Yellow Shirts resumed mass rallies. Meanwhile, the Democrat Party disrupted parliamentary sessions scheduled to consider the reconciliation legislation. On 1 June, the PAD blockaded parliament, forcing the first reading of the reconciliation bills to be adjourned. Later that day, in another unsupportable ruling, judges ordered parliament to delay a proposed constitutional amendment bill pending a decision on whether attempts to alter the charter undermined 'democracy with the king as head of state'. Faced with this clearly coordinated campaign of mass street protests, Democrat Party obstructionism and partisan judicial interference, Thaksin and Pheu Thai backed down, putting the reconciliation and constitutional amendment bills on hold. Stunned by the establishment's refusal to let him climb the mountain to political supremacy, Thaksin scrambled to jump back in the Red Shirts' boat. In a speech by video link on 2 June, he apologized for his earlier 'incomplete message' and condemned the double standards of the elite.

In July 2012, Bhumibol and Sirikit suffered severe health crises that ended their ability to play an active role in Thai political scheming. Bhumibol had another minor stroke; attempts to treat him led to a subarachnoid haemorrhage. Sirikit tried to exploit his condition to have herself appointed regent, but on 21 July she collapsed in the grounds of Siriraj Hospital after suffering a stroke, which left her unable to move or talk for several days afterwards. It quickly became clear that Sirikit was severely incapacitated, and doctors said she would never make a full recovery. She was unable to walk and her speech was badly affected. There was no realistic prospect that she could resume a prominent role in the establishment's struggle against Thaksin and Vajiralongkorn. It was inconceivable that she could ever be regent. The whole plan had fallen apart.

In 2013, both sides tried once again to secure their dominance in twenty-first century Thailand. Since his efforts to placate the establishment had failed, Thaksin sought to intimidate the Democrats into abandoning their opposition to an amnesty by using the Department of Special Investigation, Thailand's equivalent of the FBI, to launch a legal offensive against opposition leaders Abhisit and Suthep. Meanwhile, the traditional establishment began gearing up for another attempt to sabotage electoral democracy and overthrow the Yingluck government, backed by large donations from the Chinese Thai business elite. Their plan was to topple the elected government by the end of the year. With Sirikit incapacitated, the elite reverted to their older plan of putting Sirindhorn on the throne when Bhumibol died, either as monarch or as regent. With both the king and the queen incommunicado in hospital, it was difficult for leading members of the oligarchy to claim their plans had royal backing, so they arranged a charade to try to convince their patronage networks, and the country as a whole, that Bhumibol and Sirikit were still united and still calling the shots. In late July, palace courtiers announced that the royal couple had made a remarkable recovery from their respective ailments and no longer needed in-patient hospital treatment. Sirikit's thinning white hair was dyed jet black and a hairpiece was fitted to make her appear less dishevelled. On 1 August, the royal couple were taken out of Siriraj in a VW van and driven to the royal summer palace in the seaside resort of Hua Hin. Both of them were clearly decrepit and disorientated, staring blankly out of the van's windows as it drove past crowds of flag-waving Thais who had assembled for the supposedly joyful event. Sirikit waved mechanically with her left hand, evidence that she remained paralysed on her right side. Doctors at Siriraj dishonestly told the media that both Bhumibol and Sirikit were able to walk unaided but had been taken from their hospital beds to the van in wheelchairs as a precautionary measure to preserve their strength. The episode was another pantomime – once again the elite were exploiting the palace to give themselves spurious legitimacy. The most haunting images of the day were photographs showing Sirikit gazing uncomprehendingly out of the van's window, her face frozen in an eerie rictus.

Meanwhile, Thaksin was led into a trap. In back-channel communications, he was tricked into believing that the establishment
would accept an amnesty that brought him home. At 4 a.m. on 1
November, after several manoeuvres to thwart the spoiling tactics
of the Democrat Party, Pheu Thai used its dominant position
in parliament to push through an amnesty bill that would give
blanket forgiveness to all officials and military officers responsible for the crackdown in April and May 2010, and also absolve
Thaksin of his 2008 corruption conviction. It was a disastrous
misstep. The proposed amnesty was condemned by Thais across
the political spectrum, and galvanized middle-class outrage in
Bangkok. Thousands of protesters began taking to the streets
wearing the red, white and blue colours of the Thai flag and
blowing whistles to symbolize their contempt for the government. Stung by the strength of the popular outcry, Yingluck
abandoned the bill. But the protests did not end. The establishment's plan was not only to deny amnesty to Thaksin, but to
seek the overthrow of the elected government and the suspension
of democracy, so they could control parliament indefinitely and
sabotage Vajiralongkorn's succession when Bhumibol died.

Democrat Party politician Suthep Thaugsuban became the
public face of the protest movement. He was a curious choice
to lead a campaign supposedly demanding clean governance.
In the 1990s he had abused land reform provisions to benefit
wealthy families in Phuket, instead of the ordinary farmers the
scheme was supposed to help, causing a scandal that brought
down the government in 1995. A leaked US cable from 2008
stated: 'several Democrats have privately complained to us that
he engages in corrupt and unethical behavior' (08BANGKOK3712).
But suddenly one of Thailand's most notorious politicians was

pledging to clean up Thai politics and stamp out corruption, cheered on by crowds of middle-class supporters. It only made sense when viewed in the context of succession – the protesters were motivated less by outrage over the routine corruption that characterized Thai politics than by fear of a looming dark age in which Thaksin and Vajiralongkorn would dominate the country. The old elite's strategy was by now well established: they would use a campaign of street protests, parliamentary disobedience and judicial sabotage to undermine the government, just as they had in 2006 and 2008. On 20 November in one of its most extra-ordinary decisions, the Constitutional Court ruled that efforts by the government to make the upper house, the Senate, fully elected once again instead of partially appointed as it had been since the 2006 coup, were unlawful. Judges claimed that having elected senators would be less democratic, because it would allow the 'political class' to dominate the upper house. On 25 November, protesters stormed and occupied several government offices in Bangkok. Their attempted provocations escalated in the days and weeks that followed, but disciplined policing and active efforts by the government to avoid confrontation thwarted protest leaders' hopes of inciting a major confrontation that could be used as a pretext for a coup.

The protesters faced the same problem that had bedevilled every incarnation of the Yellow movement since 2005 – most Thais didn't support them. They were an anti-democratic move-ment claiming to represent Thailand's people but unable to win elections. They sought to mask this uncomfortable fact by making absurdly exaggerated claims about the number of people joining the rallies, insisting millions of people were regularly taking to the streets, whereas most international media estimated that numbers never exceeded 200,000 and were usually much lower. Repeating the same crude tactic as the coup junta in 2006, the movement adopted different names in English and Thai, to emphasize their self-proclaimed monarchism to their domestic audience while trying to conceal the royal dimension of the conflict from the foreign media. In Thai they called themselves 'The People's Committee for Absolute Democracy with the King as Head of State' and in English 'The People's Democratic Reform Committee'. The Democrat Party claimed to be independent of the movement but continued its strategy of actively sabotaging parliamentary democracy and then complaining democracy was not working. On 8 December, all of the 153 remaining Democrat Party members of parliament resigned. On 9 December the government called the bluff of the protesters, announcing a snap election to be held on 2 February.

This put Abhisit's Democrat Party and Suthep's protest movement in an embarrassing position. They knew they had no hope of winning at the polls. Adopting the slogan 'Reform Before Election', Suthep demanded that the government step down immediately and be replaced by an unelected 'People's Council' that would govern for twelve to eighteen months and formulate wide-ranging political reforms. Only then would elections be held. The protest movement was unable to provide any credible suggestions on what reform would entail, simply declaring that 'Thaksinism' had to be crushed, and that a committee of elders would work out the details later. It was the same empty promise made by every group seeking to abrogate democracy since 1932 – they would reform the country and build genuine democracy. It had never happened, and it was clear to most Thais that Suthep was hardly the person to make it happen now.

Abhisit announced that the Democrats would boycott the elections – the second time during his leadership of the party that it had refused to take part in the electoral process. The establishment defended its rejection of democracy by blaming poor voters for repeatedly electing parties controlled by Thaksin. Chitpas Bhirombhakdi, one of the protest leaders and a member of the Singha beer dynasty, declared that Thais lacked a 'true understanding of democracy ... especially in the rural areas' (Fuller, 2014). But this narrative had long been discredited – Pasuk and Baker described it as 'dangerous nonsense' (Pasuk and Baker, 2013). There was no evidence that vote-buying decisively influenced the result of elections, and plenty of evidence that it had no effect at all. The protesters blowing their whistles on the streets showed little inclination to listen to reason or evidence, however. Hard-core supporters and guards working for the protest movement sought to violently disrupt election preparations, and Suthep announced a mass protest to 'shut down Bangkok' from 13 January and prevent the elections taking place. State agencies joined efforts to topple the government: the National Anti-Corruption Commission began exploring various avenues for impeaching members of the ruling party, and the Election Commission tried to shirk its duty to organize the polls and pressed for a postponement. Princess Chulabhorn, the youngest of the king and queen's four children, began explicitly signalling her support for the protesters on social media, further eroding support for the monarchy.

The explicitly anti-democratic aims of the anti-government movement, their violent tactics and their threat to blockade the elections caused a dramatic drop in their domestic support and turned international opinion against them. The attempt to shut down Bangkok with mass protests was a failure – numbers were far lower than expected, and most middle-class protesters began to drift away. The shrinking crowds were dominated by southern Thais who had been paid to join the protests. In another clumsy attempt to win some kind of legitimacy, Suthep published an open letter to US President Barack Obama on 24 January, claiming that the government was a 'dictatorial regime' and that 'millions of people representing the whole of Thailand have risen up'. But such posturing was pointless given that his movement was actively sabotaging democratic elections and clearly did not represent the people of Thailand at all. When several Thais going to polling stations for advance voting on 26 January were assaulted by protesters, the dreadful publicity left Suthep's movement more isolated and discredited than ever. Even Thais who had never taken voting very seriously before were enraged that anti-democracy protesters were seeking to take away their rights. Defying threats of violence, blockades of polling stations, absentee election officials and all the efforts of the establishment to sabotage the election, more than 20 million Thais – 48 per cent of the electorate – managed to cast their votes on 2 February. Many more wanted to vote but found polling stations blocked or closed.

Provisional results from constituencies in which the election was not disrupted showed that Yingluck Shinawatra's Pheu Thai had easily secured enough votes to remain the dominant party in government. But because sabotage and obstruction of voting had prevented the election from being completed in several provinces – particularly in southern Thailand – the kingdom was plunged into a constitutional crisis. Yingluck remained prime minister at the head of a caretaker administration, but Thailand lacked a legitimately elected government, and it was unclear when – if ever – voting could be completed.

Meanwhile, the supposedly neutral state agencies tasked with safeguarding Thai democracy instead proceeded to dismantle it, piece by piece. On 21 March 2014, the Constitutional Court declared the election invalid, because it had not been completed in one day, a ruling widely regarded as ridiculous by independent legal experts. On 7 May, the Court forced Yingluck from office in another unsupportable judgment, finding her guilty of abuse of power because she had removed the National Security Council chief from his post in 2011. Several cabinet ministers were also ordered to step down. But the caretaker Pheu Thai government was still in office. The royalist establishment had inflicted severe damage on the caretaker administration's ability to govern, but – despite relentless constitutional chicanery – had failed to land a knockout punch that brought down the whole government. Disruptive street protests continued, but also failed to dislodge the administration. And so, as so often in Thai history, it was left to the military to deliver the killer blow to Thai democracy. After seizing power on 22 May, the junta announced it might be years before elections could be held again.

To give spurious legitimacy to their coup, the junta insisted democracy in Thailand was not working, due to the intractable positions of politicians on all sides. It was necessary, they said, to suspend elections indefinitely, so that unspecified political reforms could be enacted. But in fact, democracy had not failed in Thailand. It had been wilfully sabotaged by the traditional establishment and Suthep Thaugsuban's extremist street movement, with the acquiescence of the military. They had conspired to make Thailand ungovernable, and then used the chaos and discord they themselves had sown as a pretext for seizing power and denying Thai voters their democratic rights. Paranoid, authoritarian and repressive, the junta hunkered down to cling to power for as long as necessary to ensure they remained in charge for the royal succession when Bhumibol eventually died. The military was unable to produce any evidence that the elderly and ailing monarch approved of their coup, and it was unclear if he was even aware of what was going on in his kingdom. Thailand had become a desolate and divided place, haunted by the past and afraid of the future, waiting fearfully for its decrepit and depressive old king to finally die.

EPILOGUE

'Flip on the lights and flush out the ghosts'
What the future holds

When Bhumibol Adulyadej dies, Buddhist priests will place nine sheets of gold leaf inscribed with sacred text on the nine principal parts of his body, according to the fifteenth-century palace law that governs royalty. Members of his family and the Royal Wardrobes Department will dress his corpse in silk clothes – including gloves, socks and a hat – as well as 'heavy gold bracelets, anklets, and rings, and a golden mask ... symbolic of the radiant visage of a god'. A gold ring will be placed in his mouth. After a pause, his body will be manoeuvred into a seated position:

> The trunk is lifted, the palms joined opposite the face by means of an iron clamp, a sort of wedge is placed under the chin, and the knees are lifted to the level of the hands and tied in a sitting position. The corpse, thus seated, is placed on sixteen long strips of cotton material, the ends of which are raised and tied over the top of the head. (Quaritch Wales, 1931)

Bhumibol's personal crown will be placed on his head, and 'a heavy gold chain studded with diamonds' around his neck. Then 'the dead king ... arrayed in richer attire than he ever wore in his lifetime' will be wedged inside an inner urn 'of silver, with a lid that can be hermetically sealed', which is in turn placed inside an octagonal outer urn 'of great magnificence, being of gold ornamented with the nine gems and capped by a tapering pyramidal spire'. This will be taken to the Grand Palace and placed on a catafalque under a nine-tiered white umbrella. His body will remain inside the urn for months or years, as monks chant continuously day and night beside it and Bhumibol's favourite dishes, prepared by palace chefs, are placed in front of the catafalque at mealtimes. On set days of the week, for a few hours, ordinary Thais will be allowed to come and pay their respects (Quaritch Wales, 1931). A period of mourning will be declared. According to the US embassy: 'Public celebrations would certainly be canceled, and most Thais would find it inappropriate to attend concerts or other entertainment events, at least during the early part of the mourning period' (07BANGKOK5718). Until the reign of Rama IV it was compulsory for all Thais to shave their heads during the mourning period, but this practice has been discontinued.

As the king's corpse decomposes, its fluids will gradually leak out of the urn. Quaritch Wales described the mechanics of the process in his account of past royal embalmments:

> The base of the inner Urn is in the form of an iron grating, and from the outer Urn a copper tube passed down into the hollow catafalque where the depositions accumulated in a golden vase. Access to the interior of the catafalque was obtained by means of a small door on the western face, and each alternate day until the corpse was dry and no further liquids dripped from the tube, that is to say until about two months after death, an attendant entered and removed the vase. (Quaritch Wales, 1931)

A huge funeral pyre, symbolizing Mount Meru, will be built in Sanam Luang, the park beside the Grand Palace. In past centuries the pyre was surrounded by a host of other temporary buildings, including 'a large refreshment hall where all except the lowest classes could obtain food and drinks without charge; stands for the letting off of fireworks; and a great variety of theatrical entertainments and other side-shows'. However, according to Quaritch Wales, 'With the exception of the refreshment hall, all these were abolished in accordance with the wish of King Rama V, who considered that such celebrations did not harmonize with the dignity which ought to characterize the royal obsequies.'

On the designated cremation day, the king's body will be removed from the urn, and all the clothes and gold ornaments removed. In past cremations, wrote Quaritch Wales, 'Only the bones remained, and these, if they fell to pieces, were rearranged in the form of a human skeleton.' After being washed in coconut water, the bones will be tied up in a white cloth and replaced in the inner urn, which will be carried on a palanquin and taken to the 'Great Funeral Car', a wheeled vehicle pulled by attendants. A huge procession of soldiers, palace officials and priests, some blowing conch shells, will accompany the urn to the funeral pyre. The urn will be placed in the pyre, and at sunset the new monarch will light a symbolic fire. This moment will be 'greeted by the roar of cannon, a fanfare of trumpets, and the playing of the National Anthem'. Around 10 p.m., the ceremonial fire burning at the top of the pyre will be allowed to spread and consume the whole structure. The following morning, holy water will be poured on the ashes, which will be 'given roughly the form of a human figure with the head turned towards the east', then 'stirred up and reformed with the head turned towards the west', and finally stirred up and faced towards the east again – symbolizing 'the rising, setting, and again rising of the sun' and 'birth, death, and rebirth'. Relics of Bhumibol's body will be collected, perfumed and preserved. The whole spectacle is designed to demonstrate the grandeur of royalty and pretend that kings never really die:

It is particularly important that a Royal Cremation should be celebrated with the greatest possible pomp, because death is the greatest danger that the idea of divine kingship has to combat. It strikes right at the roots of the whole conception, and instils doubt into the minds of a people who, until recently, had not dared even to contemplate the possibility of a king suffering from any mortal infliction; and now, with the spread of western education, modern scepticism, and the shadow of communism, the Royal Cremation plays an even bigger part than formerly in impressing on the people that the king is not dead, but has migrated to a higher plane, where he will work out his destiny as a Bodhisattva for the good of all beings. (Quaritch Wales, 1931)

The ceremonies for Bhumibol's death and cremation will be little different to the rituals enacted centuries ago in Ayutthaya. Much else about Thailand's contemporary crisis has echoes in the distant past, too.

Throughout Thai history, the looming death of the king has unleashed conflict and scheming among the elite as they struggle to ensure the next monarch is somebody they can control. The establishment's desperate efforts to prevent Vajiralongkorn becoming King Rama X have dominated elite-level politics since 2005. The prospect of Thaksin and the crown prince using the vast wealth of the Crown Property Bureau to transform Thailand and elevate a new ruling class at the expense of the old terrifies the oligarchy that runs the country. Throughout his reign, Bhumibol was a pliant and mostly powerless monarch who tended to do what he was told. Vajiralongkorn, in alliance with Thaksin, would be a very different prospect. The old elite would no longer be able to use insider palace deals and royal patronage to maintain – and sanctify – their dominance. Not only would they lose access to the economic advantages conferred by the favouritism of the Crown Property Bureau, but they would also no longer be able to draw on the social status and political influence that derive from perceived closeness to the palace. Thaksin, if he succeeds in playing kingmaker for Vajiralongkorn, hopes to be richly rewarded. He is as obsessed by royal succession as his opponents. Fixated on their own narrow self-interest, Thaksin and the old establishment are waging a fight to the death, ignoring the aspirations of ordinary Thais. Both sides have sought to provoke killings and chaos as part of their strategy. Both sides have systematically undermined the rule of law and sought to co-opt institutions that should be impartial. Neither side appears to care how much collateral damage they cause. Thailand's economy has been stunted by years of conflict, and the livelihoods of most of its people have suffered. The country has become bitterly polarized, with communities and families riven by animosity. The rights of ordinary Thais have been repeatedly denied.

This elite war of succession will rage until Bhumibol dies. There is no prospect of any deal or accommodation between the feuding factions ending the crisis, because neither side can trust the other to keep its promises when the succession happens. For the leading figures behind the elite struggle against Thaksin and Vajiralongkorn, there is no way back now. They have committed themselves, and the losers in the conflict will be mercilessly crushed by the winning side. As Chairat Charoensin-o-larn says, Thai politics have gone 'beyond the point of accommodation': 'Each side is waiting for the right moment to wage a total war to eradicate the other side in the conflict in order to set up a hegemony' (Chairat, 2013). And so, for as long as the king remains alive, Thailand will be convulsed by chronic instability. US ambassador Eric John warned in 2008: 'The political turmoil may well persist for years, until the passing of the King and the subsequent redefinition of the place of the monarchy in 21st century Thailand' (08BANGKOK3289). A Credit Suisse research report in January 2014 predicted that 'street protests and frequent changes of government could scar the political landscape for several more years' (Fineman and Siriporn, 2014). These gloomy forecasts are realistic. Thailand's medium-term future looks extremely bleak.

The same forces that drove the rise and decline of Southeast Asian kingdoms throughout the past millennium are at work in twenty-first century Thailand. The power struggles of the elite have dramatically weakened the fabric of the centralized Bangkok state and caused a crisis of legitimacy for the monarchy. Insurgency and resistance in ethnic Malay Muslim communities in southern Thailand have intensified. In the old kingdom of Lanna in northern Thailand, and in the Isaan region in the north-east, talk of secession has become increasingly common. More than 20,000 rural communities have declared themselves 'Red villages', pledging their loyalty to Thaksin. The monarchy is openly criticized by villagers in these communities, an extraordinary change from their overwhelming royalism just a decade ago. The mandala state is shrinking. Thailand is unravelling at the edges.

Since 2006, Thailand's traditional elite have inflicted one disaster after another upon themselves and the country. Their efforts to sabotage the succession by suppressing popular sovereignty have stirred anger and resentment among millions of ordinary Thais, but they seem intent on continuing to pursue this disastrous strategy. They have failed to grasp that if they keep removing elected governments they will face a popular uprising by Thais who refuse to accept their rights being repeatedly denied and their votes routinely ignored. The people of twenty-first-century Thailand will not allow democracy to be taken away without a fight.

The longer the military holds power without allowing free and fair elections, the higher the risk that significant civil unrest will erupt. The only way the elite can hope to impose their will on an increasingly restive population is through force. Hard-line members of the Thai elite are actively discussing such a scenario, emboldened by events in Cairo in 2013 when the Egyptian military demonstrated that even in the era of social media and global news coverage an army can crush civilian opposition if it is willing to be brutal enough and ignore international opinion. But given the ideological divisions and factionalism within the Thai army, it is unlikely to be either willing or able to enforce the dominance of the old establishment. The military has killed far more Thais than enemy combatants over the past century, but if soldiers are told to turn their guns on their own people once again, many may refuse to do so this time. Thailand's military would probably split, and the country would tumble into civil war. Army leaders are unlikely to risk such a scenario. The attempted assassination of Thaksin or Vajiralongkorn, or some of their leading allies, is increasingly likely as the old establishment grows more isolated and desperate. Wild talk of kidnap and assassination has become increasingly commonplace among the ruling class. A few bullets, they believe, could fix the situation once and for all.

As the elite drag Thailand deeper into conflict, discussion of their war over the succession remains criminalized. Use of the *lèse-majesté* law to silence debate and dissent has dramatically escalated since 2006. The unpredictability and apparent arbitrariness of who gets hit with *lèse-majesté* charges, and the grotesquely disproportionate punishments they usually receive, recall the random eruptions of royal violence and cruelty in Ayutthaya centuries ago. The intended psychological impact on the population is the same: the establishment hopes to inculcate fear and obedience by making an example of the unlucky few and destroying their lives. But they are fighting a losing battle: the *lèse-majesté* law has become a profound embarrassment for Thailand; despite blocking hundreds of thousands of web pages, the authorities have been unable to prevent discussion of the monarchy and succession, particularly on social media. Draconian enforcement of the law is likely to persist until well after the royal succession – both sides in the conflict over the throne want to use the law to suppress scrutiny of their actions.

There is no doubt that Bhumibol's death will be traumatic for the millions of Thais who genuinely revere their king. Millions more, who have already lost faith in the monarchy and no longer support it, are likely to feel grave anxiety, due to widespread expectations that the succession will unleash a period of severe conflict and instability. But in fact, while it is highly possible that violence will erupt in the days and weeks after Rama IX dies, it is likely to lead to a period of greater stability. Thailand cannot be at peace while he is alive. Only his death can bring the kingdom's crisis towards a resolution.

The longer Bhumibol survives, the greater the chance that Vajiralongkorn becomes King Rama X without a significant challenge. Most of the succession conflict will have already been fought, before his death rather than after. Bhumibol could also ensure his son succeeds him by abdicating before he dies and proclaiming Vajiralongkorn his chosen heir. But the likelihood of the king taking active steps to influence events has diminished to almost zero – he appears too incapacitated and too unaware of what is happening to make a decisive intervention. His most regular companion is his favourite daughter Sirindhorn, long the favoured choice of Thailand's people to become the next monarch. For most of her life, she went out of her way to signal she had no intention of challenging her brother – she never married, never had children, and spread word that she would retire to a special residential compound near Beijing after Bhumibol's death. 'A majority of royal watchers we have talked to, including many who know her well, predict she will quietly leave the country once her father passes, for both the stability of the country and her own personal safety, leaving the Thai stage to her brother', stated a secret US cable from 2009 (09BANGKOK2967). However, Sirindhorn began explicitly signalling support for anti-government protests in late 2013, although less clumsily than her younger sister Chulabhorn, and royal sources confirm she backs efforts to block Vajiralongkorn becoming king. Given her unique position as the closest person to Bhumibol, she is well placed to control the information he receives and also to misrepresent his purported wishes after he dies. The king was socially isolated throughout his reign, which made him easy to manipulate. This is even more the case as he approaches his death.

Assuming enemies of Vajiralongkorn remain in control of the privy council and the military, then when Bhumibol dies a contested succession is highly probable. Sirindhorn and her allies will attempt to keep news of the king's death secret for as long as possible, and will probably keep him artificially breathing on a respirator, to give them time to prepare a decisive strike against the crown prince. It will require an element of constitutional chicanery – some legalistic basis will have to be found to justify blocking Vajiralongkorn, perhaps by falsely claiming that the king left instructions on a posthumous change to his choice of heir, or invoking Article 10 of the 1924 Palace Law, or leaking details of crimes allegedly committed by the prince or diseases he is believed to suffer from to justify claims that he is unfit to reign. There will also have to be a military element to the plan; Vajiralongkorn is aware the royal succession is likely to be contested and has been quietly consolidating power over the past decade, putting allies in important ministries and institutions, and expanding his personal force of soldiers who report directly to him. He is ready to fight for his right to reign if necessary. Thailand's military would need to quickly find a way to neutralize the crown prince's forces – and perhaps capture or even kill him. After that, some way would need to be found to ensure parliament formally approved their alternative candidate for monarch. And all of this needs to happen quickly. If the plan hits a roadblock, for a few days or even a few hours, it is likely to fall apart and Vajiralongkorn will be king.

The probability of a challenge to the crown prince is dismissed by many analysts because of the damage it would do to a monarchy already haemorrhaging legitimacy and popular support. What they fail to understand is that the Thai ruling class do not want a strong, politically independent palace – they want a monarch they can manage. The prospect of Thailand becoming a genuine constitutional monarchy after Bhumibol's death, with a powerless ceremonial king or queen, is far more acceptable to the traditional elite than the risk of an aggressive and vengeful monarch who hates them. They want to remain in control of the immense fortune of the Crown Property Bureau, and they want to continue to bask in the aura of royal patronage, even if the palace is a shadow of what it once was. Their nightmare is not a weakened monarchy; it is a hostile monarch who refuses to serve their interests.

An extremely long mourning period is likely to be announced after Bhumibol dies. The most plausible forecast is 999 days, given the symbolic importance of the number nine in the iconography of Bhumibol's reign. The palace propaganda machine will be cranked up to full blast, with the military and the establishment attempting to manipulate the genuine grief of millions of Thais to conceal succession machinations and try to use Bhumibol's exalted reputation to legitimize whatever arrangements they engineer afterwards. As Peter Jackson has argued, Bhumibol has already become a 'virtual deity' – to his followers, he is a magical semi-divine figure, and the ruling class have long planned to exploit his sacred aura even years after his death (Jackson, 2009). But this is no longer a viable possibility in twenty-first-century Thailand: too many people have lost faith in the monarchy since the 2006 coup, and after Bhumibol dies all his secrets will finally spill out – his accidental killing of his brother, his involvement in the events that led to the 1976 Thammasat massacre, his acquiescence to the 2006 coup, and his lifelong hostility to democracy. Bhumibol is no longer a unifying figure in Thailand. The elite cannot rely on his aura to protect them after he dies.

Once the succession question is decided decisively – through the victory of the crown prince or an alternative candidate – then political progress will become possible once again. The likeliest scenario is that Thaksin and Vajiralongkorn emerge victorious. If this happens, their opponents will finally understand the suicidal stupidity of the strategy they have adopted since 2005. The appropriate way to prepare for the rule of a populist strongman like Thaksin and a monarch like Vajiralongkorn, as some members of the establishment appeared to grasp in the 1990s, was to strengthen democracy and the state institutions that act as checks and balances to executive power, entrench the rule of law, and allow freedom of speech. Instead, they have done exactly the reverse. If Thaksin and Vajiralongkorn prove to be the kind of rulers the old establishment fear they will be, then the tables will suddenly turn on those who conspired to eviscerate Thai democracy, turn the judiciary and state institutions into partisan tools of the powerful, and use the *lèse-majesté* law to silence dissent. The authoritarian twisted Thailand they have created will remain, but they will no longer be its masters.

If the old elite somehow find a way to win, and put an alternative monarch on the throne, the prognosis for Thai democracy is no better. They will seek to do what they have always done: monopolize power via extra-constitutional methods, and deny Thailand's people the right to determine their own destiny.

But, despite all the reasons for pessimism, there is cause for hope in twenty-first-century Thailand. The most extraordinary change of the past decade is that Thailand's poor have developed sophisticated political consciousness and become aware of what is wrong with their country. They understand the games the ruling class have played throughout history, and they are no longer willing to play. They want real democracy and they want their rights to be respected. They will not take no for an answer.

In July 2006, the embattled Thaksin Shinawatra told America's ambassador over a steak lunch in an expensive Bangkok restaurant that he was sick of a sclerotic unelected elite running Thailand behind the scenes, and 'wanted to flip on the lights and flush out the ghosts' (06BANGKOK4041). Whatever his political future, whether he returns in triumph to rule Thailand or dies in exile a defeated man, Thaksin's ensuring contribution to his country is that the lights are now on, and the ghosts have nowhere to hide. The future may be uncertain and frightening for many Thais. But for a country cursed by the legacy of its history, just looking to the future at all – and talking about it openly – represents a victory over the dead hand of the past.

References

ARTICLES AND BOOKS

Abhisit Vejjajiva (2013) *The Simple Truth*, Post Publishing, Bangkok.
AFP (2013) 'Thai Opposition Torn between Elections and "People's Revolution"', 16 December.
Aikman, David (1976) 'A Nightmare of Lynching and Burning', *Time*, 18 October.
Altman, Howard (2002) 'The King of BLING BLING', *American Journalism Review*, September.
Anderson, Benedict R. O'G. (1977) 'Withdrawal Symptoms: Social and Cultural Aspects of the October 6 Coup', *Bulletin of Concerned Asian Scholars*, vol. 9, no. 3, pp. 13–31.
——— (1978) 'Studies of the Thai State: The State of Thai Studies', in Eliezer B. Ayal (ed.), *The Study of Thailand*, Ohio Center for International Studies, Athens OH, pp. 193–247.
——— (2012) 'Outsider View of Thai Politics', www.prachatai.com/english/node/2694; accessed 7 February 2014.
Askew, Marc (2010) 'Confrontation and Crisis in Thailand 2008–2010', in Marc Askew (ed.), *Legitimacy Crisis in Thailand*, Silkworm Books, Chiang Mai, pp. 31–82.
Baker, Chris (2006) 'Revival, Renewal and Reinvention: The Complex Life of Thailand's Monarch', www.asiasentinel.com/society/revival-renewal-and-reinvention-the-complex-life-of-thailands-monarch; accessed 7 February 2014.
——— (2008) *The Revolt of Khun Phaen*, paper presented at the 10th International Conference on Thai Studies, Thammasat University.
Bangkok Post (1991) 'Page One Comment', 16 November.
——— (2010) 'Red Rage Rising', 13 March.
Batson, Benjamin (1974) *Documents from the End of the Absolute Monarchy*, Cornell Data Paper No 96, Cornell University Press, Ithaca NY.
Battye, Noel (1974) 'The Military, Government and Society in Siam, 1868–1910', Ph.D. thesis, Cornell University, Ithaca NY.

Bechstedt, Hans-Dieter (1991) 'Identity and Authority in Thailand', in Craig J. Reynolds (ed.), *National Identity and Its Defenders*, Silkworm Books, Chiang Mai.

Bhumibol Adulyadej (1997) *The Story of Mahajanaka*, Amarin, Bangkok.

—— (2002) *The Story of Tongdaeng*, Amarin, Bangkok.

Bishop, Ryan, and Lillian S. Robinson (1998) *Night Market: Sexual Cultures and the Thai Economic Miracle*, Routledge, London and New York.

Borwornsak Uwanno (2006) 'Ten Principles of a Righteous King and the King of Thailand', paper published by Faculty of Law, Chulalongkorn University, Bangkok.

Bowie, Katherine (1997) *Rituals of National Loyalty: An Anthropology of the State and the Village Scout Movement in Thailand*, Columbia University Press, New York.

—— (2008) 'Vote Buying and Village Outrage in an Election in Northern Thailand: Recent Legal Reforms in Historical Context', *Journal of Asian Studies*, vol. 67, no. 2, pp. 469–511.

Boyle, Peter (2010) 'Red Shirt Leader on New Stage in Fight', *Green Left Weekly* 856.

Branigan, Tania (2000) 'Bangkok Prince Orders a Thai Takeaway – From Warwickshire', *Guardian*, 11 November.

Callahan, William A. (2005) 'The Discourse of Vote Buying and Political Reform in Thailand', *Pacific Affairs*, vol. 78, no. 1, pp. 95–113.

Chairat Charoensin-o-larn (2013) 'Thailand in 2012: A Year of Truth, Reconciliation and Continued Divide', in Daljit Sing (ed.), *Southeast Asian Affairs 2013*, Institute of Southeast Asian Studies, Singapore, pp. 287–306.

Chalathip Thirasoonthrakul (2008) 'Thai Queen Weighs in with Anti-govt Protesters', Reuters, 13 October.

Chamberlain, James Robert (1991) *The Ram Khamhaeng Controversy: Collected Papers*, Siam Society, Bangkok.

'Chang Noi' (2006) 'The Persistent Myth of the "Good" Coup', *The Nation*, 2 October.

Chanida Chitbundid (2007) *The Royal Projects: The Establishment of Royal Hegemony*, Foundation for the Promotion of Social Science and Humanities, Bangkok.

Chatthip Nartsupha (1984) 'The Ideology of 'Holy Men' Revolts in North East Thailand', in Andrew Turton and Shigeharu Tanabe (eds), *History and Peasant Consciousness in South East Asia*, National Museum of Ethnology, Osaka.

Chula Chakrabongse (1960) *Lords of Life*, Taplinger, New York.

Connors, Michael Kelly (2008) 'Article of Faith: The Failure of Royal Liberalism in Thailand', *Journal of Contemporary Asia*, vol. 38, no. 1, pp. 143–65.

—— (2011) 'Thailand's Emergency State: Struggles and Transformations', in Daljit Sing (ed.), *Southeast Asian Affairs 2011*, Institute of Southeast Asian Studies, Singapore, pp. 287–305.

Crispin, Shawn W. (2007) 'Recollections, Revelations of a Protest Leader', *Asia Times*, www.atimes.com/atimes/Southeast_Asia/ID27Ae01.html; accessed 7 February 2014.

Crosette, Barbara (1987) 'Once Upon a Time a Good King Had 4 Children...', *New York Times*, 15 December.

—— (1989) 'King Bhumibol's Reign', *New York Times*, 21 May.

Dhani Nivats (1947) 'The Old Siamese Conception of the Monarchy', *Journal of the Siam Society*, vol. 36, no. 2, pp. 91–104.

Educational Technique Bureau (1978) *Studybook Preparing for the Experience of Life*, Department of Education, Bangkok.

Englehart, Neil A. (2001) *Culture and Power in Traditional Siamese Government*, Cornell University Department of Asian Studies, Southeast Asia Program Series No. 18, Cornell University Press, Ithaca NY.

English, Khaosod (2014) 'Army Unveils Song "Authored By Gen. Prayuth"', http://en.khaosod.co.th/detail.php?newsid=1402215513, accessed 9 June 2014.

Far Eastern Economic Review (2002) 'A Right Royal Headache', 10 January.

Ferrara, Federico (2012) 'The Legend of King Prajadhipok: Tall Tales and Stubborn Facts on the Seventh Reign in Siam', *Journal of Southeast Asian Studies*, vol. 43, no. 1, pp. 4–31.

—— (2014) *Thailand's Unfinished National Revolution: Kings, Coups, and Constitutions since 1932*, Cambridge University Press, Cambridge.

Fineman, Dan, and Siriporn Sothikul (2014) 'Thailand Market Strategy', Credit Suisse, 7 January.

Fuller, Thomas (2014) 'Thai Beer Loses Esteem after Heiress's Remarks', *New York Times*, 10 January.

Geertz, Clifford (1980) *Negara: The Theatre State in Nineteenth Century Bali*, Princeton University Press, Princeton NJ.

Gervaise, Nicolas (1928) *The Natural and Political History of Siam*, trans. Herbert Stanley O'Neill, Siam Observer Press, Bangkok.

Gesick, Lorraine (1983) 'The Rise and Fall of King Taksin: A Drama of Buddhist Kingship', in L. Gesick, (ed.), *Centers, Symbols and Hierarchies: Essays on the Classical States of Southeast Asia*, Yale University Southeast Asian Studies, New Haven CT.

Glassman, Jim (2004) *Thailand at the Margins: Internationalization of the State and the Transformation of Labour*, Oxford University Press, Oxford.

Good, Paul (2000) Interview for the Foreign Affairs Oral History Project,

Association for Diplomatic Studies and Training, www.adst.org/OH%20 TOCs/Good,%20Paul.toc.pdf; accessed 7 February 2014.

Gray, Christine Elizabeth (1986) 'Thailand: The Soteriological State in the 1970s', Ph.D. thesis, University of Chicago.

Grossman, Nicholas, and Dominic Faulder (2011) *King Bhumibol Adulyadej: A Life's Work*, Editions Didier Millet, Singapore.

Grow, Mary Louise (1991) 'Laughter for Spirits, a Vow Fulfilled: The Comic Performance of Thailand's lakhon chatri Dance-drama', Ph.D. thesis, University of Wisconsin-Madison.

Handley, Paul M. (2006a) *The King Never Smiles: A Biography of Thailand's Bhumibol Adulyadej*, Yale University Press, New Haven CT.

—— (2006b) 'What The Thai Coup Was Really About', *Asia Sentinel*, 6 November, www.asiasentinel.com/politics/what-the-thai-coup-was-really-about; accessed 7 February 2014

Heine-Geldern, Robert (1956) *Conceptions of State and Kingship in Southeast Asia*, Cornell University Department of Asian Studies, Southeast Asia Program Data Paper No. 18, Ithaca NY.

Hobsbawm, Eric (1986) 'Introduction: Inventing Traditions', in Eric Hobsbawm and Terence Ranger (eds), *The Invention of Tradition*, Cambridge University Press, Cambridge.

Human Rights Watch (2011) *Descent into Chaos*, www.hrw.org/sites/default/files/reports/thailand0511webwcover_0.pdf; accessed 7 February 2014.

Iyer, Pico (1988) 'The Smiling Lures of Thailand', *Time*, 17 October.

Jackson, Peter A. (2004a) 'The Thai Regime of Images', *Sojourn: Journal of Social Issues in Southeast Asia*, vol. 19, no. 2, pp. 181–218.

—— (2004b) 'The Performative State: Semi-coloniality and the Tyranny of Images in Modern Thailand', *Sojourn: Journal of Social Issues in Southeast Asia*, vol. 19, no. 2, pp. 219–53.

—— (2009) 'Markets, Media, and Magic: Thailand's Monarch as a 'Virtual Deity', *Inter-Asia Cultural Studies*, vol. 10, no. 3, pp. 361–80.

Jory, Patrick (2002) 'The Vessantara Jataka, Barami, and the Bodhisatta-Kings: The Oorigin and Spread of a Thai Concept of Power', *Crossroads: An Interdisciplinary Journal of Southeast Asian Studies*, vol. 16, no. 2, pp. 36–78.

Junya 'Lek' Yimprasert (2010) 'Why I Don't Love the King', www.academia.edu/487133/Why_I_dont_Love_the_King; accessed 7 February 2014.

Kasian Tejapira (2001) *Commodifying Marxism: The Formation of Modern Thai Radical Culture, 1927–1958*, Kyoto University Press, Kyoto.

—— (2006) 'Toppling Thaksin', *New Left Review* 39.

Kemp, Jeremy (1969) *Aspects of Siamese Kingship in the Seventeenth Century*, Social Science Association Press, Bangkok.

—— (1978) 'Cognatic Descent and the Generation of Social Stratification in Southeast Asia', *Bijdragen tot de Taal-, Land- en Volkenkunde*, vol. 134, no. 1, pp. 63–83.

—— (1984) 'The Manipulation of Personal Relationships: From Kinship to Patron-Clientage', in Han ten Brummelhuis and Jeremy Kemp (eds), *Strategies and Structures in Thai Society,* University of Amsterdam, Antropologisch-Sociolgisch Centrum, Amsterdam.

Kershaw, Roger (2001) *Monarchy in South East Asia: The Faces of Tradition in Transition*, Routledge, London and New York.

Keyes, Charles F. (1977) 'Millennialism, Theravada Buddhism, and Thai Society', *Journal of Asian Studies*, vol. 36, no. 2, pp. 283–302.

—— (2006) 'The Destruction of a Shrine to Brahma in Bangkok and the Fall of Thaksin Shinawatra: The Occult and the Thai Coup in Thailand of September 2006', Asia Research Institute Working Paper Series, No. 80.

Khaosod English (2014) 'Army Unveils Song 'Authored By Gen. Prayuth', http://en.khaosod.co.th/detail.php?newsid=1402215513, accessed 9 June 2014.

Klima, Alan (2002) *The Funeral Casino: Meditation, Massacre, and Exchange with the Dead in Thailand*, Princeton University Press, Princeton NJ.

Kobkua Suwannathat-Pian (2003) *Kings, Country and Constitutions: Thailand's Political Development 1932–2000*, Routledge, New York.

Kullada Kesbonchoo Mead (2004) *The Rise and Decline of Thai Absolutism*, Routledge, London and New York.

Lady Gaga (2012), https://twitter.com/ladygaga/status/205265026016223232; accessed 7 February 2014

Lloyd Parry, Richard (2009) 'Thaksin Shinawatra: The Full Transcript of His Interview with The Times', *The Times*, 9 November.

Loos, Tamara (2005) 'Sex in the Inner City', *Journal of Asian Studies*, vol. 64, no. 4, pp. 881–909.

Malinowski, B. (1925) 'Magic, Science and Religion', in Joseph Needham (ed.), *Science, Religion and Reality*, Macmillan, New York, pp. 19–84.

Mallet, Marian (1978) 'Causes and Consequences of the October '76 Coup', *Journal of Contemporary Asia*, vol. 8, no. 1, pp. 80–103.

Marquez, Xavier (2013) 'A Model of Cults of Personality', APSA 2013 Annual Meeting Paper.

Marshall, Andrew MacGregor (2013) 'Thailand's Saddest Secret', www.zenjournalist.org/2013/03/06/thailands-saddest-secret.

McBeth, John (1986) 'Voice of the Palace: The Royal Family Denies Some Persistent Rumours', *Far Eastern Economic Review*, vol. 133, no. 36.

McCargo, Duncan (2001) 'Populism and Reformism in Contemporary Thailand', *South East Asia Research*, vol. 9, no. 1, pp. 89–107.

—— (2005) 'Network Monarchy and Legitimacy Crises in Thailand', *Pacific Review*, vol. 18, no. 4, pp. 499–519.

—— (2008) 'Thailand: State of Anxiety', *Southeast Asian Affairs 2008*, Institute of South East Asian Studies, Singapore.

—— (2009) 'Thai Politics as Reality TV', *Journal of Asian Studies*, vol. 68, no. 1, pp. 7–19.

McCarthy, Terry (1999) 'The King and Ire', *Time*, 6 December.

McManus, Jason (1966) 'Holder of the Kingdom, Strength of the Land', *Time*, 27 May

Ministry of Foreign Affairs (2009) 'Gist of PM Abhisit Vejjajiva's Address at the Foreign Correspondents Club, Hong Kong (FCCHK), 15 May 2009 and Q&A Session', www.mfa.go.th/main/en/media-center/28/1618–Gist-of-PM-Abhisit-Vejjajivas-Address-at-the-Forei.html; accessed 7 February 2014.

—— (2010) 'Frequently Asked Questions about the Current Political Situation in Thailand', www.thaiembassy.sg/press_media/press-releases/frequently-asked-questions-about-the-current-political-situation-in-thail; accessed 7 February 2014.

—— (2011) 'FAQ', www.thailandtoday.org/monarchy/faq; accessed 30 September 2013.

Morell, David, and Chai-anan Samudavinija (1981) *Political Conflict in Thailand*, Oelgeschlager, Gunn & Hain, Cambridge MA.

Morris, Rosalind C. (2000) *In the Place of Origins: Modernity and Its Mediums in Northern Thailand*, Duke University Press, Durham NC.

Murashima, Eiji (1988) 'The Origin of Modern Official State Ideology in Thailand', *Journal of Southeast Asian Studies*, vol. 19, no. 1, pp. 80–96.

Murray, David (1996) *Angels and Devils*, Orchid Press, Bangkok.

Natapoll Chaiching (2010) 'The Monarchy and the Royalist Movement in Modern Thai Politics, 1932–1957', in Søren Ivarsson and Lotte Isager (eds), *Saying the Unsayable: Monarchy and Democracy in Thailand*, NIAS Press, Copenhagen.

The Nation (1992) 'Suchinda's Second Coup', 8 April.

—— (2006a) 'Vandal's Dad Distraught', 23 March.

—— (2006b) 'Thaksin Era Beset by Evil Omens', 22 March.

—— (2006c) 'HM the King Suggests a Solution', 27 April.

—— (2007) 'Samak Declares Victory and Is Ready to be PM', 24 December.

—— (2008a) 'Bloodbath in Bangkok', 8 October.

—— (2008b) 'A Coup via TV?', 17 October.

New York Times (1932) 'Prophecy Supported by Siamese Overturn', 25 June.

—— (1935) 'King Prajadhipok of Siam Abdicates Because Democracy is Rejected', 4 March.

—— (1969) 'Long Thai Dispute over Estate Ends', 6 April.

Nostitz, Nick (2008) 'What Happened on 7/10/2008?', *Prachatai*, www.prachatai.com/english/node/830; accessed 7 February 2014.

—— (2009) *Red vs. Yellow*, Volume 1: *Thailand's Crisis of Identity*, White Lotus, Bangkok.

—— (2011a) *Red vs. Yellow*, Volume 2: *Thailand's Political Awakening*, White Lotus, Bangkok.

—— (2011b) online comments, http://asiapacific.anu.edu.au/newmandala/2011/07/05/who-ordered-the-killing; accessed 7 February 2014.

O'Kane, John (1972) *The Ship of Sulaiman*, Routledge & Kegan Paul, London.

Olson, Martha Stevenson (1999) 'A Train Called Betsy Debuts in Bangkok', *New York Times*, 26 December.

Pasuk Phongpaichit and Chris Baker (2009a) *A History of Thailand*, 2nd edn, Cambridge University Press, Cambridge.

—— (2009b) *Thaksin*, Silkworm Books, Chiang Mai.

—— (2013) 'Vote-buying Claims Nothing but Dangerous Nonsense', *Bangkok Post*, 6 December.

Pasuk Phongpaichit and Sungsidh Piriyarangsan (1994) *Corruption and Democracy in Thailand*, Silkworm Books, Chiang Mai.

Peagam, Norman (1975) 'Probing the "Red Drum" Atrocities', *Far Eastern Economic Review*, 14 March.

Peleggi, Maurizio (2002) *Lords of Things: The Fashioning of the Siamese Monarchy's Modern Image*, University of Hawaii Press, Honolulu.

—— (2009) 'Thailand in Crisis: The Twilight of a Reign or the Birth of a New Order?' Asia Research Institute Working Paper No. 114, National University of Singapore.

Petchanet Pratruangkrai (2012) 'Govt Complains to US Embassy over Lady Gaga', *The Nation*, 29 May.

Porphant Ouyyanont (2008) 'The Crown Property Bureau in Thailand and the Crisis of 1997', *Journal of Contemporary Asia*, vol. 38, no. 1, pp. 166–89.

Pravit Rojanaphruk (2010) 'Red Tide Returns', *The Nation*, 20 September.

—— (2012) 'Court Defers Lese Majeste Case, defence advised', *The Nation*, 20 July.

Pridi Banomyong (2000) *Pridi by Pridi*, Silkworm Books, Chiang Mai.

Quaritch Wales, H.G. (1931) *Siamese State Ceremonies*, Bernard Quaritch, London.

Scott, James C. (2009) *The Art of Not Being Governed: An Anarchist History of Upland Southeast Asia*, Yale University Press, New Haven CT.

Shah, Sudha (2012) *The King In Exile*, HarperCollins, New Delhi.

Smithies, Michael (1995) *Descriptions of Old Siam*, Oxford University Press, Kuala Lumpur.

Solomon, Robert L. (1970) *Aspects of State, Kingship and Succession in Southeast Asia*, Rand Corporation, Santa Monica.

Stanton, John (1950) 'Garden of Smiles', *Time*, 3 April.
Stent, James (2010) 'Thoughts on Thailand's Turmoil', www.zenjournalist. com/2010/06/thoughts-on-thailands-turmoil-by-james-stent; accessed 7 February 2014.
Stevenson, William (1999) *The Revolutionary King*, Constable, London.
Streckfuss, David (2011) *Truth on Trial in Thailand: Defamation, Treason, and Lèse-Majesté*, Routledge, London and New York.
Streckfuss, David, and Thanapol Eawsakul (2009) 'Speaking the Unspeakable: Lese-Majeste and the Monarchy in Thailand', http://thaipoliticalprisoners.files.wordpress.com/2009/01/streckfuss-and-thanapol.pdf; accessed 7 February 2014.
Stowe, Judith (1991) *Siam Becomes Thailand: A Story of Intrigue*, University of Hawaii Press, Honolulu.
Sukhumbhand Paribatra (1988) 'Apprehension about the Future', *Far Eastern Economic Review*, 21 January.
Sulak Sivaraksa (1992) 'Would This Man Dis the King? A Conversation with Sulak Sivaraksa', *Fellowship USA*, vol. 59, no. 9.
—— (2000) *Powers That Be: Pridi Banomyong through the Rise and Fall of Thai Democracy*, Lantern Books, Bangkok.
Suthichai Yoon (2006) 'Old Soldiers Never Die; They Raise "Career" Thoroughbreds', *The Star Online*, www.thestar.com.my/story.aspx/?file =%2f2006%2f7%2f23%2fasia%2f14907851&sec=asia; accessed 7 February 2014.
—— (2009) 'Piya Malakul, the Dinner Host, Said there was No Talk of Coup', *The Nation Blog*, http://blog.nationmultimedia.com/ThaiTalk/ 2009/03/29/entry-1; accessed 7 February 2014.
Tanabe, Shigeharu (1984) 'Ideological Practice in Peasant Rebellions: Siam at the Turn of the Twentieth Century', in Andrew Turton and Shigeharu Tanabe (eds), *History and Peasant Consciousness in South East Asia*, National Museum of Ethnology, Osaka.
Tansubhapo, Thanida, and Wassana Nanuam (2014) 'Prayuth to Broadcast "Happiness"', *Bangkok Post*, 1 June.
Ten Kate, Daniel (2012) 'Thai King's Advisers Key to Lese-Majeste Reform, Thaksin Says', Bloomberg News, 25 September.
Terwiel, B.J. (1979) 'Tattooing in Thailand's History', *Journal of the Royal Asiatic Society of Great Britain and Ireland* 2, pp. 156–66.
—— (2011) *Thailand's Political History from the 13th Century to Recent Times*, River Books Press, Bangkok.
Thak Chaloemtiara (2007) *Thailand: The Politics of Despotic Paternalism*, Silkworm Books, Chiang Mai.
Thanida Tansubhapol and Wassana Nanuam (2014) 'Prayuth to Broadcast "Happiness"', *Bangkok* Post, 1 June.

Thongchai Winichakul (1994) *Siam Mapped*, University of Hawaii Press, Honolulu.

—— (1995) '*Jodmai Chaebob Thi Neung* (Letter Number One)', in *Rao Mai Leum Hok Tula* (*We Do Not Forget October 6*), 20th Anniversary Memorial Publication, Bangkok.

—— (2000) 'The Quest for "Siwilai": A Geographical Discourse of Civilisation Thinking in Late Nineteenth and Early Twentieth Century Siam', *Journal of Asian Studies*, vol. 59, no. 3, pp. 528–49.

—— (2002) 'Remembering/Silencing the Traumatic Past: The Ambivalent Memories of the October 1976 Massacre in Bangkok', in Shigeharu Tanabe and Charles F. Keyes (eds), *Cultural Crisis and Social Memory*, University of Hawaii Press, Honolulu.

—— (2004) 'A Short History of the Long Memory of the Thai Nation', paper presented at the Asian Nationalism Project, 1–3 October.

—— (2008) 'Toppling Democracy', *Journal of Contemporary Asia*, vol. 38, no. 1, pp. 11–37.

—— (2011) 'Foreword', in Tyrell Haberkorn, *Revolution Interrupted: Farmers, Students, Law, and Violence in Northern Thailand*, University of Wisconsin Press, Madison.

Time (1955) 'Orchids for the Secretary', 28 February.

—— (1992) 'The King and Them', 1 June.

Tulsathit Taptim (2008) 'Saving Private Abhisit', *The Nation Blog*, www.nationmultimedia.com/2008/12/09/headlines/headlines_30090182.php; accessed 7 February 2014.

Turton, Andrew (1984) 'Limits of Ideological Domination and the Formation of Social Consciousness', in Andrew Turton and Shigeharu Tanabe (eds), *History and Peasant Consciousness in South East Asia*, National Museum of Ethnology, Osaka.

Ünaldi, Serhat (2013) 'Working Towards the Monarchy and Its Discontents: Anti-Royal Graffiti in Downtown Bangkok', *Journal of Contemporary Asia*, vol. 44, no. 2, pp. 377–403.

Van Beek, Steve (ed.) (1983), *Kukrit Pramoj: His Wit and Wisdom*, Editions Duang Kamol, Bangkok.

Van Der Cruysse, Dirk (2002) *Siam and the West: 1500–1700*, Silkworm Books, Chiang Mai.

Van Vliet, Jeremias (1910) *Description of the Kingdom of Siam*, trans. J.F. Ravenswaay, Siam Society, Bangkok.

—— (2005) 'Diary of the Picnic Incident', in Chris Baker, Dhiravat na Pombejra, Alfons Van Der Kraan and David K. Wyatt (eds), *Van Vliet's Siam*, Silkworm Books, Chiang Mai.

Vithoon Amorn (2010) 'Thai King's Health Has Improved, Queen Says', Reuters, 11 August.

Walker, Andrew (2008) 'Dishonourable but Parliamentary', *New Mandala*, http://asiapacific.anu.edu.au/newmandala/2008/12/09/dishonourable-but-parliamentary; accessed 7 February 2014.

—— 'Prayuth's Threat' (2011) *New Mandala*, http://asiapacific.anu.edu.au/newmandala/2011/06/16/prayuths-threat; accessed 7 February 2014.

—— (2012) *Thailand's Political Peasants*, University of Wisconsin Press, Madison.

Washington Post (1992) 'The King and They', 23 May.

Watts, David (1983) 'A Backward Step for Democracy', 7 April.

Weber, Max (1962) *Economy and Society*, Bedminster Press, New York.

Wolters, O.W. (1982) *History, Culture and Region in Southeast Asian Perspectives*, Institute of Southeast Asian Studies, Singapore.

Wood, W.A.R. (1926) *A History of Siam*, T. Fisher Unwin, London.

Wright, Michael (1995) 'A Pious Fable: Reconsidering the Inscription I Controversy', *Journal of the Siam Society*, vol. 83, nos 1 and 2, pp. 93–102.

Wyatt, David K. (2003) *Thailand: A Short History*, 2nd edn, Yale University Press, New Haven CT.

Ziegler, Philip (1985) *Mountbatten: The Official Biography*, Knopf, New York.

Zimmerman, Gereon (1967) 'A Visit with the King and Queen of Thailand', *Look*, June 27.

Žižek, Slavoj (2011) 'Good Manners in the Age of WikiLeaks', *London Review of Books*, vol. 33, no. 2, pp. 9–10.

US DIPLOMATIC CABLES

611.90/10–2059
Available at http://history.state.gov/historicaldocuments/frus1958–60v15/d534
1975BANGKO18375
Available at http://aad.archives.gov/aad/createpdf?rid=315747&dt=2476&dl=1345
05BANGKOK2219
05BANGKOK7197
06BANGKOK1767
06BANGKOK2149
06BANGKOK2990
06BANGKOK3180
06BANGKOK6085
06BANGKOK3538
06BANGKOK3916
06BANGKOK4041
06BANGKOK5429

06BANGKOK5929
07BANGKOK311
07BANGKOK712
07BANGKOK940
07BANGKOK2280
07BANGKOK5718
07BANGKOK5738
07BANGKOK5839
08BANGKOK198
08BANGKOK1293
08BANGKOK2610
08BANGKOK3042
08BANGKOK3289
08BANGKOK3317
08BANGKOK3712
08BANGKOK3774
09BANGKOK325
09BANGKOK974
09BANGKOK2167
09BANGKOK2342
09BANGKOK2455
09BANGKOK2606
09BANGKOK2967
09BANGKOK3067
10BANGKOK192
10BANGKOK340
10BANGKOK380
10BANGKOK478
Available at http://wikileaks.org/origin/174_0.html.

Index